MW01596180

What othe
From The Dad's Corner

"I love this." **- Clyde Gray – Newscaster – WCPO – Channel 9**

"What a MARVELOUS book - I'm flattered to be in such company – including yours. What a terrific project." **- Jack Atherton - Newscaster – WLWT - Channel 5**

"This book is AWESOME - I am honored and will be glad to participate." **- Alfonso Cornejo – President – Hispanic Chamber USA**

"Regardless of our age or of our children's age, this book is a valuable resource to help us to continue to hone our skills as a father." **- Pat Leary – International Business Consultant**

"It brought tears to my eyes." **– Ray Dishman – Assistant Fire Chief**

"This book is very inspiring and truly a treasure – I thoroughly enjoyed it." **Dee Lorenz – Health Ministries**

"One of the greatest gifts I could give to my children." **– Susan Hornsby – Mother**

"Every Father should be writing a page." **– James Shelton – Retail Manager**

"This book is so motivational and inspiring that it should be in all Jr. High and Sr. High schools." **– Malinda Humphries – Teacher**

What others are saying about
From The Dad's Corner

"I'm loving this incredibly powerful book – lots of emotions have come out while reading it – this is such a beautiful book." **Robin Quallick – Daughter**

"I wish I had a page from my own father." **– Jack Davidson – Construction Supervisor**

"This book is so wonderful and powerful that I'm giving one to each of my own grandchildren." **– Diana McClure – Grandmother**

"This is great!!" **- Andrew Stapleton – Computer Analyst**

"Thank you again for taking the time to prepare such profound and memorable pages." **- Conrad Stephenson - Realtor**

"I am inspired by the content and, even at my age, I continue to learn from what the other fathers have to say." **- Jack Greenfield – Retired Pilot**

"This book will help my children in so many ways." **- Angela Tracy - Single Mom**

"It takes a village to raise a child – and this book provides many allies to achieve just that." **- Thomas Holland – Professor**

From The Dad's Corner

60 outstanding fathers share with their own sons and daughters their deepest and most intimate thoughts on life's lessons.

R. K. Ketterer

From The Dad's Corner
Alexandria, KY

From The Dad's Corner

From The Dad's Corner Publishing
19 Spillman Drive
Alexandria, KY 41001

ISBN - Soft Cover 978-0-9881875-0-4

Library of Congress Control Number 2012946967

A THOUGHT FROM THE DAD'S CORNER

"The young always have the same problem – how to rebel and conform at the same time. They have now solved this by defying their parents and copying one another."

Quentin Crisp

About the Author

The author of *From the Dad's Corner* is a single father who raised two beautiful daughters.

Attended: University of Wisconsin, University of Kentucky, Northern Kentucky University, Ohio College of Applied Science. Bachelor of Science – Business Management

35 years as a corporate manager in telecommunications

Producer of award-winning cable television show – *Entertainers in the Tri-State* 21 nominations – 12 awards in Cultural Awareness – Diversity – Community Action – Entertainment – Documentary – Performing Arts

Producer – *Stars of Magic* production

Motivational Speaker, Author, Real Estate investor, and Entertainer/Magician

A word from the Author

Why Write This Book?

Often, we fathers feel like we have less influence in our children's lives than we would like. This book is another way to reach them: a way to assure that our children don't miss any important messages about life that we may have for them; just another way to share our feelings with them; to let them know that we love them and that we are proud of them.

Sometimes it's not the message but the messenger. Sometimes it takes many messengers to deliver the same message before it is received and accepted. Sometimes it is not what is said but who says it. And sometimes the timing is just not right for the person to receive the message. Through this book, the information has a better chance of being available when our children are ready to receive our messages. So from that perspective this may be considered a reference book to life.

I have discussed this topic with fathers from many walks of life, fathers of various ages, fathers from many parts of the country, and one common thread continues to surface.

Nearly every father echoes the same dismay: *My children just don't want to listen to me. I don't have a voice. They shut me down. They shut me out. I can't get through to them.*

Many agree that the most obvious and noticeable period of this behavior is between the early teens and through the mid to late twenties. This really comes as no surprise to most, especially to Mark Twain, as he is remembered by his famous quotation. "When I was a boy of 14, my father was so ignorant I could hardly stand to have the old man around. But when I got to be 21, I was astonished at how much the old man had learned in seven years."

So what is this mysterious force that makes children turn away from their fathers' advice and guidance?

Perhaps it is the children's need to grow up – to search for independence – basically saying, "Look, Dad, I don't need you – I can do this on my own." Perhaps they are searching for that respect of being a strong independent adult.

Or perhaps the advice that fathers are giving them is simply just what they don't want to hear. They want to do it their way for the immediate self-gratification and are not considering the consequences of their decisions.

Or perhaps they legitimately want to go in a different direction than what the father believes is right or good for them.

Or perhaps it is the approach that the father is taking to communicate. Often how the message is delivered determines how it is received.

Or perhaps, or perhaps, or….

But one desire, for sure, shared by many good fathers is that their children would at least just listen to them.

Good fathers are not trying to keep their children from growing up. Actually what they want is very basic – they want their children to experience a good life – one better than they had. They want their children to live a balanced life, being self-assured, and being triumphant in their pursuits. They want them to have meaningful, long-term relationships and have good morals and ethics throughout their lives.

So 60 good fathers have come together to allow the readers to peek into their private thoughts and words, words that they share with their own children-- like Reality TV (a good version) in a book. They are talking to their own children – not to you – not to me, and we are permitted to listen in and be enlightened by these conversations. Our children and the readers of this book will take away some insights and values that focus on the blessings that enrich our lives. These pages from the fathers will help minimize some of life's difficulties, problems, and heartaches.

Good fathers want their children to live a healthy, happy, and rewarding life.

A THOUGHT FROM THE DAD'S CORNER
"If you have knowledge, let others light their candles from it."
Margaret Fuller (1810 – 1850)

DEDICATION

As the author, I would like to dedicate this book to the five most important people in my life.

To:
My parents- Charles Ketterer (now deceased) and Alice – who have carried out a lifelong commitment to being dedicated parents and who both have lived by an incredible work ethic, which they have instilled in their five children.

My daughters- Robin (Ketterer) Quallick and Katie Ketterer – who have taught me more about life than I could ever teach them. They have allowed me to enjoy the wonderful blessings and endure the difficult challenges that come with being a father. They have inspired this book.

My dearest friend- Regina Katherine Hellyer – who is my significant other; she has enriched my life in so many ways, brought me happiness, has taken me to new heights and taught me how to enjoy life.

A THOUGHT FROM THE DAD'S CORNER
"Don't ever give up. Don't ever give in. Don't ever stop trying. Don't ever sell out. And if you find yourself succumbing to one of the above for a brief moment, pick yourself up, brush yourself off, whisper a prayer, and start where you left off. But never, ever, ever give up." **Richelle Goodrich, Eena, The Two Sisters**

ACKNOWLEDGMENTS

This project started off very small but quickly grew to include many different people. It became an intense labor of commitment and took the combined efforts of many to accomplish this remarkable book. I wish to acknowledge the following:

Regina Katherine Hellyer
For her endless typing, transcribing, editing; her patience with me as I focused on this time consuming and powerful project; and her encouragement through the challenging times.

60 Outstanding Fathers
For taking their time to gather their thoughts and submit wonderful pages and for being willing to share their deepest ideas and experiences on life's lessons.

Tom Bemmes (page 24) and **Richard Osterlind** (page 112)
For contributing their valuable experiences in publishing, offering direction, and sharing their positive outlook on life.

A THOUGHT FROM THE DAD'S CORNER

"Knowledge is in the end is based on acknowledgement."
                              Ludwig Wittgenstein

TABLE OF CONTENTS

FORWARD

By Clyde Gray / Newscaster

Here is why I think guys are saying, "yes" to this project. There is such an orientation in our society to hearing what women think about things - particularly about child rearing and what a mother hopes for and dreams for her children. And that is worthy because it is an important part of what every child needs to have.

What we lack, however, is the opportunity for fathers to vent their emotions and their feelings about their children. The standard view of fathers is that we are often remote, chilly, inaccessible, often focused on work and seldom ever giving enough thoughts to the emotional needs of our children, when a point in fact is that many of us quietly do, in the way that men do, ache everyday for being away from our children for whatever amount of time we are, for being separated from them by divorce or other circumstance, such as military deployment or what have you.

What some folks don't understand is that many fathers carry around a certain amount of grief in their hearts when they are away from their children, but inside is a deep and abiding passion and love for their children that just never really gets tapped.

So when you say to a father, "What do you want to say to your kids and other children who may be reading this?"- Boom, here we go!

DISCLAIMER

The contents of this book are directed by and based upon good fathers – fathers that do everything they can for the betterment of their children. But let's face it. Not every father is a good one.

Defining what makes a good father is not always easy – perhaps it is easier to define what is *not* a good father. We hear of hostile and terrible acts coming from some fathers:
Some fathers do horrible and bad things to their children.
Some fathers skip out of their responsibilities as a parent.
Some fathers appear to be the pillars of society and yet at home they have a whole different raging personality.

Defining a good father is not easy and often only those in the immediate family really know what the truth actually is.

When we encourage children to follow their parents' guidance, we are referring explicitly to good parents.

A THOUGHT FROM THE DAD'S CORNER
"Plato is my friend, Aristotle is my friend, but my greatest friend is truth." **Sir Isaac Newton**

INTRODUCTION

"When I was a boy of 14, my father was so ignorant I could hardly stand to have the old man around. But when I got to be 21, I was astonished at how much the old man had learned in seven years."

                                                    Mark Twain

Most fathers, sooner or later, become the victim of the "Just Dad" syndrome. I know of fathers that hold very powerful and prestigious positions in the corporate world but at home – they're "Just Dad." As a result they often have a limited number of words. Yes, they can say more, and often do, but once their invisible allowance of words is reached, the walls go up and the children tune out most everything that Dad says after that.

This book provides those good fathers with the opportunity to communicate and share their thoughts. It gives them a voice – a record of their words. (And possibly a few more extra words than they might otherwise have in their own environment.)

In the pages that follow you will be exposed to the wisdom, the values, the guidance, the perceptions, different experiences, and advice that are shared by various good fathers in many different walks of life. Watch for uniqueness as well as similarities and patterns.

The intentions are pure. There are no hidden agendas. It's advice that many different good fathers are giving to their own sons or daughters. It's an accumulation of more that 3,500 years of experience. It's the single compilation of the truest and most openhearted information available to pass on to you and to generations to come.

To my two incredible daughters of age 22 and 24,

Know that: I love you more than words can ever say and I am so very proud of you both. I have treasured every minute of being your father and I cannot imagine my life any other way. Know that I will always be there for you and I will continue to savor the joys that you bring to me.

The top values that I encourage for you are:

POSSESSIONS
Make sure your possessions serve you and you are not a slave to your possessions –
The more you own the more they own you. Don't be a pack rat.

IDENTITY
What you do when no one is looking defines you –
How you treat those less fortunate than you – those that need help – is a good barometer of your character –
Never turn down good help but never expect someone to carry your weight if you are capable. Take care of yourself. Don't rely on someone else to take care of you (unless you truly can't). You are responsible for your own happiness: no one else is responsible for that. So don't let anyone steal your joy. There will always be people ahead of you as well as people behind you. Be a conduit of humanity.

EDUCATION - LEARNING
Learn – Learn fast – learn easy (to learn from your mistakes is great but to learn from someone else's mistakes is genius) just learn – some people never learn – if it is not working for you – take a step back – figure out what you are doing wrong (notice I said you) and try a new approach – Never stop learning. When you stop learning – you stop living. Live to learn – learn to live. Your Degrees, Diplomas, and certifications are your passport to travel the fast track of life. They indicate you have the "Right Stuff". Education is one of the best

investments you can make – you receive a lifetime of returns. So Read – Read More – Then Read Some More –

UNDERSTAND THE RULES OF LIFE – OF SOCIETY

You seldom get to make the rules – but understanding the rules often makes you a better player. Life is not fair – Society is not Fair – Not everyone is for you – Not everyone that you think is your friend is truly your friend. Be aware that very few will ever help you surpass them – including your sibling. Don't ever give up your power. Understand your heritage: the responsibilities of your parents, of yourselves, of your children-to-be. Understand where you've come from and where you are going.

Love,
Dad

Anonymous
Born 1959

A THOUGHT FROM THE DAD'S CORNER
"You learn more quickly under the guidance of experienced teachers. You waste a lot of time going down blind alleys if you have no one to lead you." **W. Somerset Maughham, The Razor's Edge, 1943**

To my two sons, David age 34, and Jeff age 31,

Know that: I love you so much. I am so proud of you and you fellows have really made my life something special. Mom and I always look forward to being with you and being a part of your life. We are proud of your accomplishments. Dave, you have really excelled, and we are proud of you for all the things that you do, and how you are going into management with Fidelity. Jeff, you are picking up the rear here, but you are doing a great job too; we know you are going to go places with ZF.

The top values that I encourage for you are:

KEEP GOD FIRST
Fellows, I think the most important thing for your life is to keep God first in your life and to look forward to a special relationship with the Lord. I know, Jeff, you are a little bit hesitant on that but you will come around, and you will see in days to come that the Lord is a vital part of you life. And, Dave, I am glad that you and your family are in church and are involved in church, and are growing, and we like what is going on there. We are just so proud of you fellows.

CONTINUE YOUR EDUCATION
Jeff, I pray that someday you and April will settle down and tie the knot. I know that you love her, but you are still hesitant on taking the big step due to your past. You are doing a good job. Zaylee is something special and we just love her to pieces. We thank you for doing a good job with her and being a good young man. We want you to continue your education and go forward. I know that you are doing well in school now, and the company is spending good money on training you. You will go forward with ZF and do a fine job for them. We need to get your finances in order and you will come around.

BALANCE AND ATTITUDE
Fellows, you both have good lives now, and we just pray you will go forward with a good balance in your lives and good attitudes. It will take you everywhere.

CHARACTER AND INTEGRITY
Remember your character and your integrity are the most important things you can have. Take care of your name and protect it. Be sure to honor your name and your word, foremost and above all things. Remember that you have to take a stand for things because if you don't stand for something then you will fall for anything.

Love, Dad!

Larry Alexander
Born 1952
Thomas More College
Career: IRS
Hobbies: Videos, Church work, fishing

A THOUGHT FROM THE DAD'S CORNER
"Learning is not attained by chance, it must be sought for with ardor and attended to with diligence."
Abigail Adams, 1780 – US wife of John Adams 1764 (1744 – 1818)

To my Dearest Alexandra of age 23,

Know that: I am so very proud of your academic accomplishments, and continue to be amazed at the level to which you have grown and matured as a young adult. You have had worldly adventures that your parents and grandparents did not have the opportunity to experience. I hope that with your expanded visions of world events and exposure to different social cultures, you share these realities with others through your field of Journalism (or other paths you choose throughout life), and that these help you to make good choices for betterment of both your physical and spiritual self.

May you have a long, healthy, and happy life, filled with positive memories and learning from each walk along your path. May you find fulfillment and enlightenment from each experience. And may you know family and friends who provide sustenance, love and caring to you, as you as well provide such sustenance, love and caring to them.

The top values that I encourage for you are:

FOLLOW YOUR DREAMS

I encourage you to follow your dreams, to the extent that the guiding light which brightens your path provides sufficient economic and spiritual sustenance to fulfill both your basic and emotional needs and desires. However, recognize that in life you will approach many crossroads and at each point you have the opportunity to continue on the same path or vary onto an alternative path. Be flexible and willing to explore opportunities along these many paths in your physical and spiritual journeys.

FAMILY AND FRIENDS

Keep all of your family members and friends close to your heart, and show by your words and actions that you care and are compassionate toward others despite human frailties that will surface from time to time. Know that truths and revelations will continue to surface and be discovered; each discovery and newly revised outlook on life will provide you with boundless opportunities to explore and further understand why people act in various ways. With this knowledge, try to anticipate and prepare for ongoing life changes, yet realize that some occurrences will be beyond your physical control and yet, may be within your emotional control.

CHOICES AND GOALS

As mentioned in my last birthday message to you, the choices you make daily include how you decide to present and define yourself to other people. Relationship building is a key component of success, so continue to expand your circle to include people who bring positive energy and enthusiasm into daily living. Consider creating flexible short-term and long-term plans for yourself, and take focused actions to move toward achievement of such goals. Yet, realize that some of the most insightful concepts will be learned from areas where success was not achieved; so don't be afraid to try new things as each endeavor will provide new wisdom from the action taken and results achieved.

With all my love, and all my heart,
Dad

Charles Arkin - Born: 1957
Education:
  Doctorate of Law (IIT-Kent, Chicago)
  Masters in Intl Business (Roosevelt)
  Bachelor in Finance and Economics
    (University of Illinois – Chicago)
Married to Lori since April 2010
Career: Lawyer, Contracts Manager,
  College Instructor, Finance & Econ.,
  Director of Credit,
  Director of Operations
Hobbies and interests:
  Magician and Escape Artist
  Volunteer, Cincinnati Legal Aid Society
  Eagle Scout
  Vigil Order of the Arrow

To my two daughters, Gray (who is 24) and Chase (who is 19),

Know that: I am tremendously proud of you, not least because you have taken wonderful chances in life, and -- rightly or wrongly! – you have heeded some of my advice.

The top values that I encouraged for you are:

IDENTITY
I have told you both since you were little that you don't have to succumb to peer pressure, and you don't have to feel stuck in this particular moment in time. What makes us human is our ability to live across the ages and to choose only the best of what has come before, and to build upon it. So the fact that people in our time are wearing jeans and getting tattoos and listening to certain kinds of music doesn't mean that you have to. You of course can, if you so choose: but you can also enjoy Mozart and Beethoven and find your own style.

LIVE LIFE TO ITS FULLEST
You can be time-travelers living in all eras and across all boundaries. And, taking that advice, you both have traveled the world. You are much more intrepid and more questing than I was at your age (or even now). I'd like to think that is because your mother and I really tried to empower you and make you feel that the world is something for you to conquer and for you to relish, and that history is not musty and dusty but a treasure trove for you.

ROLE MODEL
The hero in my life, and the person I have hoped will always be the hero in yours, is your mother. She married a lawyer in New York City, but she helped me to find the courage to leave the bar, which I did not find very fulfilling, and to go into the entirely different and very precarious broadcasting

profession. Mama gallivanted with me across the country --
to San Antonio and Miami, Florida, and finally (and this was
the greatest gift to us) here to Cincinnati—the best place in
the world to bring up children. She went out and worked so
that we could send you to private schools, and so we could
put you through universities without having to incur any
debt. Mama has risen to great heights in her own profession
of marketing. She is simply an outstanding mother and
professional and, best of all, wife, and I hope you will be just
like her -- but with a better husband!

All my love,
Dad

Jack Atherton
Born: 1952
Married to Aymsley for 30 years
Studied History at Yale and law at
Columbia University – Masters in
Journalism at Columbia - Practiced
corporate litigation in Manhattan –
Published editorial Cartoons, Reviews
of classical music and books –
KENS(CBS)-San Antonio,
WTVJ(NBC)-Miami, WXIX-Cincinnati,
WLWT-Cincinnati
Hobbies: classical music and reading
the Great Books

To my three children Jamie, Kristie, and Brian, who are between the ages of 22 and 27,

Know that: I love you very much and I want the very, very best for you. So here are some thoughts that I have discovered in my life that will help you during yours.

The top values that I encourage for you are:

KEEP GOD FIRST IN YOUR LIFE

Most importantly, keep God first in your life. Trust Him and be open to His awesome unconditional love! Know that our sole purpose in life is our SOUL purpose! Our goal is to become the very best version of ourselves. To be our best self we must prepare & train. To start, always remember that God is the perfect master and you are one of His masterpieces! You are a beautiful, unique, special, perfect being! God is always with you, feel His presence at every moment and allow His love to fill you completely! With TOTAL love, you will always completely forgive. Forgiveness is giving love when there is no reason to. Forgive others, yourself and God. Don't take anything personally. Always remember that those who deserve love the least, need it the most! Stop telling God how big your mountains are and start telling your mountains how big your God is!! When you choose God and accept His love, you will be in heaven here on earth!

HEALTH

The next most important thing in life is your Health! Health comes from what goes into your mouth and in your mind. Guard carefully all that enters! Choose harmony, peace & joy. Slow down, take time to meditate, focus on the great things that are all around us! Live in the moment, yesterday is history, tomorrow is a mystery, today is a gift and that is why we call it the present! This very moment is all we have; choose to see beauty, to feel beauty, to experience beauty! Soak it in, then share it!

CHARACTER & INTEGRITY

Add to your faith and health, Character & Integrity. If you have character & integrity nothing else matters, if you don't have character & integrity nothing else matters! You

are the writer, director and producer of your life! You are
limitless! Take responsibility for every choice you make!
To change some things in your life, you must change
some things in your life! To change your life, change your
thoughts! Set goals and dream big. You are worthy of all
your dreams! Aim for the right target; run the right race;
satisfy the soul! Be impeccable with your thoughts &
words, they create your reality! To make your goals and
dreams come true, you must take action, what actions
are you taking TODAY to get closer to your goals and
dreams? Along the ways there will always be challenges,
embrace the challenges, for they can make you wiser,
stronger and better! Stand up for what is right yet, be a
part of the solution, loving all and building people up.

LAUGH OFTEN
Grandpa B. said: Life is too short to be unhappy; laugh
often; wake up each day with a smile on your face and
love in your heart; keep a positive attitude and optimism
is knowing that everything is beautiful, even the ugly! His
words have been a great help to me.

GUIDANCE & INTUITION
Finally, follow your inner guidance/intuition. Do not make
excuses; do not blame; do not make assumptions; do not
judge! Rather, see with your heart; listen with your heart
and follow your heart!!
Be thankful. Be grateful. Pray continuously. And always
ask: What would Jesus do?

***Do not try to change the world; change yourself and
that will change the world!***   All my love, Dad

Tom Bemmes
BORN: 1961
EDUCATION:
Urbana University BA,
Miami University-Masters
CAREER: Educator & Entertainer
HOBBIES: Magic

To my daughters Corinne of age 32 and Julia of age 28,

Know that: you are my life. You have given me a lot of reasons to go to work everyday and a lot of reasons that I didn't like going to work everyday. Like life is in general—it's bittersweet---children bring a lot of joy and they also bring a lot of worry. For me that translates into stress but I love you very much. Now that you are older and on your own, I actually want to go on working and contributing more for you than for myself. I want to try to leave a little piece of the world a little more stable for you than maybe it was for me or as I perceived it was.

The top values that I encourage for you are:
PERSEVERANCE
The greatest value I can share with you is that when things are going rough is to just continue to grind it out. There will be a lot of days when that is all you can do-- just grind it out, and eventually it will all work out. In other words, don't panic. One of the biggest things is try not to go into the self-pity type mode. Hang-in there and things will generally get better. I think a lot of people give up before they should. Like they say, you give up before The Miracle happens. That is one of the biggest lessons I have learned in life.
THE NEXT RIGHT THING
One of the other things I have always carried in the back of my mind about life—not that I always do the next right thing—is that I think there are some natural laws that are not always obvious and, if you try to do the next right thing, it seems that, in the long run, you will get back that grace: it will come back to you in a better way. I don't know where I got that from, but I believe in that. It has kept me going. I think that a lot of times I might not have kept going otherwise.
FINANACES
In finances, my biggest mistake was probably not doing some kind of planning early on. I always thought that I could do it on my own and could take care of the money situation. If you can find reputable people to deal with

then, in the long run, you will probably be better off. The whole issue of money is such a volatile issue especially in relationships. For example, your mother and I will stress about several dollars as if it is someone else's money when in reality, all our money is in one pot. It plays such a big role in marital problems. In terms of trying to control your finances, planning, asking for assistance, and getting solid financial advice would be my strongest recommendations.

FAMILY

My last thought is if you have kids and start raising a family then you will experience some unbelievable highs and probably some unbelievable lows. But in the long run, the joy of children, and especially grandchildren, overwhelms any downside. When you get older you look back, and if you do have grandchildren, that grandchild will negate probably the worst day you ever spent in your entire life. So, the parenthood stresses and worries, though sometimes quite intrusive, are definitely worth it and will, invariably, lead a family to a joy that there is no other way to obtain in life. No money, what so ever, can buy that joy.

Love, Dad!

Dr. Glenn Bichlmeir, MD
Born 1950
General Practitioner
Family Practice
Education: Dr. Bichlmeir attended medical school at University of Louisville School of Medicine and graduated in 1975 now having 37 years experience. Additional Family Practice training was conducted at St Elizabeth Medical Center.
Married to Connie for 32 years
Hobbies and interest:
Model radio-control airplanes

To my determined son of age 18 and strong minded daughter of age 23,

Know that I love you so very much. You both are determined and strong-minded individuals. I want the best for you: to be happy, to be independent, to give back to society, to be healthy and to be loved and respected. I am so proud of you both and you both have brought me so much joy.

The top values that I encourage for you are:

DREAMS AND GOALS
Set SMART (Specific – Measurable – Achievable – Realistic – Time sensitive) goals. Set high goals – you usually can achieve much more than you think.
Don't follow someone else's dreams – be inspired by them – respect their successes but don't be intimidated by them – Don't play someone's else's game – you won't beat them at their own game - play your own game and play it well. Dream BIG: Dream in COLOR.

DEVELOP A PLAN
Plan – a roadmap makes it a lot easier to get there – it's the GPS of life.
Good decisions tend to lead to a more comfortable and satisfying life.
Don't be afraid to change the plan as you go. You seldom get the plan perfect the first time.

TAKE ACTION
Do something – one small act is better than a million dreams – Dreams are great. But if you never act on them they will always be just a dream. This is where the real courage comes into play.

BE A GOOD LISTENER
You teach when you talk – You learn when you listen – So be a good listener and choose your words carefully –

LOVE GOD
Pray – Pray often – then pray some more -

FINANCE
Saving money is essential but make sure you couple that with a strong income. Combine the two and you will get the comforts and spending power that most pursue. Don't spend more than you make.

All my love,
Dad

Anonymous
Born 1963

A THOUGHT FROM THE DAD'S CORNER
"It is a paradoxical but profoundly true and important principle of life that the most likely way to reach a goal is to be aiming not at that goal itself but at some more ambitious goal beyond it." ***Arnold Toynbee (1889 – 1975)***

To my son Kaiser *of age 20,*

Know that: You are the best thing that has ever happened to me, a blessing from God, and a joy to my heart. I'm always happy with you.

The top values that I encourage for you are:

LOVE
We show you love by example and you are no stranger to the love we share in my family. As I have said on many occasions - love your siblings as my siblings and I love each other. After the old generation is gone to a better place (hopefully), all you have left for family are your siblings. Always show them love, care, and support. In return they will love you, care for you, and support you.

INTEGRITY and HONESTY
Be honest, straight forward, and ethical because your actions and how you lead your life go a long way in what you get back from life through others. A good reputation is paramount. Why do you think they let me work from home unsupervised?

WISDOM
You don't need a reminder or advice about this matter, but it is nice to keep it in mind. Be driven by passion, but don't be led by it. Follow your heart, but be sure to leave a lot of space for reason. Don't jump blindly after things; make sure logic and common sense are part of the choices you make.

BE THANKFUL
Always be thankful for the blessings that we receive from God, whether it is obvious or not, tangible or not. We take many things in our lives for granted, and we don't recognize that they were a blessing till something

happens that prevents us from enjoying them---from simple stuff as breathing comfortably to tragic accidents. Remember no matter how bad it gets, it can always be worse. Think of it as something inevitable to happen, and God was there to reduce the severity of it, like an air bag in a car that deploys to protect us.

Last words - you will always be my pride and joy.

Love,
Dad

Gabriel Bitar
Born: 1955
EDUCATION: BS Civil Engineering
CAREER: Highway/Roadway Engineer
HOBBIES: Web design, reading

A THOUGHT FROM THE DAD'S CORNER
"Only passions, great passions, can elevate the soul to great things." **Denis Diderot (1713 – 1784)**

To my two sons, Rick of age 53 and David of age 55,

Know that: when I was working with you many years ago, it was always harder for me to be objective. I was always a little harder on you, for I always expected you two to be better than the other workers. For example, if I had carpenters on the job, then you both had to be better than the other carpenters. This was because you are my sons, and I expected more of you. I know I would be "on" you more than I would be "on" the other men. And I am proud of you because of what you have done and who you have become. You both have strong abilities and manage people well. David, you are a good businessperson. You took over the business when my health was failing and ran it wisely. Ricky, you are very mechanically minded and, use good common sense too. I love you both and I believe that you know that. Your mother and I love you and we would do anything for you. If you ever need help, you know we would help you.

The top values that I encourage for you are:

FAMILY
I would like you to be happy, as happy as mom and I have been. There is nothing like having good children-- like you two have been.

CHRISTIAN FATHERS
You both are good Christian men and good fathers. I know that you would do anything for your kids, too. You pretty much picked up on what we did for you. Both of you are good fathers, maybe better than I was to you. You spend more time with your kids than I did. So much of the time, I had to work long hours each day, so your mother did most of the raising of you.

LEARN
Ricky, you once said to me, "Dad, you taught us to do everything. It helped us because now we can do

everything on a job. Some people only know how to do one thing but when we started out we did everything, concrete work, block work, brick work... everything." And the two of you do a great job.

Dave, you and Sandy have blessed us with two wonderful grandsons – Nathan and Seth. Rick, you and Peggy have blessed us with two wonderful granddaughters – Emily and Sarah. I'm proud to say that you all have seen to it that they have gotten a good education and all are successful in their chosen fields. We're proud of them and love them dearly.

FRIENDS

Friends are important to everybody. You both have always had many friends and got along well with people. Rick never met a stranger. You are both well liked.

Your mother and I are so proud of all of you. I love you both very much. And I pray that you have a good and healthy life, a happy and blessed life. God has blessed us with you two and your families. Trust in the Lord – Count your blessings and be happy.

Love, Dad

Mel Boden
Born 1931
Campbell County High School
US Air Force 4 years
15th Air force Division
Married to Thelma for 60 years
Career: Builder for 35 years

To Jami, Seth, Sara, their spouses (between the ages of 30 and 35) and my grandchildren,

Know that: I wish that you never forget that you are blessed! You were born in the United States of America, to Christian parents who love you unconditionally and you have no major health problems. Most of the world's population would gladly trade places with you. I pray that each of you will be filled with the Holy Spirit and as a result, have a life full of: love, joy, peace, patience, kindness, goodness, faithfulness, gentleness and self-control.

The top values that I encourage for you are:

DON'T PROCRASTINATE
Do what needs doing when it needs done. When faced with a huge or difficult task, remember even an elephant can be eaten but you must do it one bite at a time. If you see something that needs to be done don't wait for someone else to do it.

ANTICIPATE
Life will create enough stress for you so you don't need to create your own. Think ahead/plan. I like to use lists. Creating a prioritized list of things I need to do helps to keep me focused and working on the most important things until they are completed. I also get a sense of accomplishment and control when I am able to cross off my list the completed tasks.

Do
- Remember kids are a precious gift of God. Love them, nurture them and discipline them in a loving, compassionate manner.
- Always tell the truth and do so timely. Bad news does not get better with age!
- Live beneath your means. Trust me you will never regret doing so.
- Look people in the eye. Everyone needs/wants to feel important- especially kids.

- Say you are sorry (one of my short coming- just ask Mom- Sorry)
- Say thank you. Recognize and appreciate the efforts of others.
- Make good choices. Choose to do the right thing. Never, ever cheat. Give a lot of Thought and prayer to decisions that are irreversible.
- Listen. You have 1 mouth and 2 ears for a reason.
- Pick your battles. Some things are worthy of going to the mat for and others are not. Choose wisely.
- Put family first- especially time with the kids. They will be grown and gone before you know it. Whatever you are working on will pale in importance when you look back on the lost opportunity to spending time together.
- Pray. It works. But pray like Solomon asking for wisdom and courage - not things.

Love,
Dad

John C. Bowers
Born   1949
Education: Eastern Kentucky University- double major History Teaching and Business Administration MBA EKU Economics
Married to Linda for 40 yrs
Career - 31 years with Procter and Gamble, held various positions, retired as Senior Purchasing Manager
Hobbies- Hunting, Fishing, Reading, Working at Church, Spending time with kids and grand kids

To my two sons, Micah and Aaron, and my daughter Tara, who are between the ages of 24 and 31,

Know that: I am so very proud of you, my children. I will always love you and wish the very best of life for you, wherever you *are.*

The top values that I encourage for you are:
SPIRITUALITY
Always take the time to nourish your Spiritual side. It is always too easy to get so caught up in the cares of life, making the bills, getting to work, getting that promotion or raise that we forget to nourish the most important side of us. God created us in the beginning for company and fellowship. What a shame if we don't provide that for Him. Look around you and enjoy the magnificent creation that you are a part of. Wonder at it all as a child.
HONESTY
We are after all, only as good as our word. Let your yes be YES, and your no be NO. Don't have double standards. Treat everybody you meet and know with RESPECT. If you make a promise, keep it. If you say you will do something, do it cheerfully. Honor this to the point that NOBODY ever has reason to doubt you or your word. True honesty is this: Even when nobody else is watching, do that which you know is right, even if there is an easier way out. If you ALWAYS tell the truth, you never have to bother remembering what you have said. Truth is a very soft pillow to lay your head upon at night.
HONOR
Hand in hand with honesty, live your life with honor. Be courteous and unselfish. Tara, ALWAYS be a lady. Micah and Aaron, ALWAYS conduct yourselves as Gentlemen. It is quite OK to open a door for a lady. Protect anyone who is weaker than you. If another does NOT know the way of honor, guide him or her if you can. Live the example of honor that others can see your light shine brightly. Treat your spouse, parents, children, elders, friends, soldiers and police that protect you with honor and respect.

SLOW DOWN

What a shame to live a life and NOT take time to live. Take time to take that road you have never explored. Smell the pines and honey suckles, listen to the calls of the birds and animals around you. Take the time to sing along with your favorite songs. Make time for your spouse, family and friends. Take time to give a lot of yourself to others, because you have beauty and talent to give.

GET TO KNOW ANIMALS

I have learned so much from animals over time. Max the collie, Skipper the German Shepherd, Oscar the Boxer, Cisco the greatest horse of all, Runt and Grumpy, and Furbee the raccoons, Norbert and Precious the Squirrels. Each has taught me something. Without them, and others, life would have been much less fulfilling. Animals are just so totally honest about EVERYTHING. What they are and what they do is totally honest. They fellowship and interact with you because they want to. They know NO prejudice or wealth. I have seen Raccoons, Skunks and Opossums share the same dish happily with one another. They love you because they want to. Let animals into your heart and life and don't miss this great blessing. Animals know NO deceit. They don't expect anything in return but appreciate what you give so fully. They do not use you. Many times they will protect you. They warn you of danger you may not sense. Always be kind to them and it is almost always returned to you.

Love, Dad!

Michael J. Bray Born 1954
Police Officer
Hobbies and Interest: Music, Martial Arts, Target Shooting, Flying, Horseback Riding, Motorcycles, Fishing, Boating, Ballroom Dancing, Rollerblading, Skiing, Bicycling, Scuba Diving, Photography, Raising Orphaned Animals, Exploring nature and places I've never been before.

To Matt and Caitlin, who are between the ages of 26 and 30 years old,

Know that: you are the reason for living, that you brought such joy into my life and your mother's life, and that everyday is a blessing with you. I really mean that. Kids are funny when they are little; kids are obnoxious when they are teenagers; and then when they are older, they are funny again! Kids never leave and that is great!

The top values that I encourage for you are:

TREASURE EACH DAY
As I told you when you were growing up, never let a day go by that you don't make something good happen. When you get up in the morning, it is a gift, and the day is whatever you want to make out of it. Even when you were little and in school, I told you to make sure you learn something today that you didn't know yesterday, and make sure you do something today that's good, that you didn't do yesterday. Treat each day individually as a gift because you never know when "todays" run out. If you view each day as a gift and you view it as something that is presented to you each morning, then what are you going to do with it?

KNOW YOURSELF
We all are given certain gifts by God. My gift may be the ability to speak in front of a lot of people. But your gifts may be something completely different, but whatever gifts you have been given, figure it out, and then use your gifts to make yourself and the world a better place.

EDUCATION
Education is a big topic with me. I was a pretty lenient father as you grew up, except when it came to education. I did not want to see you slack off in school for two reasons: Number one, you would be only cheating yourselves. And two, I think I convinced you at an early age that when you went to school, that was your job and you had to do your best at your job. Eventually you would be working for someone who would expect that from you.

And, if you didn't give that to them, then you probably would have problems at that job. When it came to schoolwork, I knew it was really and truly important for you to buckle down and do your best. I know that you still talk about it today, now that you are grown adults, and hopefully you have appreciated that.

FRIENDS

I think it is very important for you to choose the right people and friends to be around in your life: good people.

FAMILY COMMUNICATION

Children look to parents for so much in terms of guidance early in life and the relationship between fathers and children is very important. Parenting is a two-way street. The relationship is nurtured by the communication back and forth between the parents and children. To me, good communication is the one thing that is critical in any kind of relationship, especially family. I think this is so important for you to do. And if you communicate well then your relationship will be so much smoother and the depth of your relationship will be so much deeper. When the time is right - talk to your children as persons, not necessarily as a child. If more of us did that, then I think parenting would be a lot less of a stressful situation and the world would be a better place.

Love, Dad

Ken Broo
Born: 1952
Native of Belleville N J
Married to Jackie for 37 years
Education: BS-Ohio University
Career: Sports Newscaster WLWT Cincinnati,
Hobbies: Sports, Collector of jukeboxes and records

To my three sons between the ages of 31 and 36,

Know that: we all were lucky to be born and even luckier to be born in the U.S. All three of you are strong, loving, and caring sons. I am so very proud of whom you have become. You are so important to me – you are my life.

The top values that I encourage for you are:

FRIENDS AND RELATIONSHIPS

I am probably the last person to be taking about this topic. I wish I had done a better job of building relationships. This takes energy and the thoughtfulness to keep them going. I sort of took them for granted; I guess I thought they would always be there. It's just like I talked about our family, you have to keep building on what you already have. It's important that you find the right people, be around positive people and people that have the same good values that you have. Being around the good people will keep you on the right path. The people that you are around will influence how you think and the things you do. Be a positive person, smile a lot; it makes the people around you feel good. Be as polite as you can; Todd is the best example of this quality that I have ever seen. Go out of your way to be nice to one person each day, compliment them, and make their day a little nicer and it will make you feel better too. These are obvious things but we don't do enough of them. Make the world a little better each day.

STARTING YOUR OWN BUSINESS

The world is not going to come to you. You have to go out and embrace the world. Some call it networking: some call it business. I believe the word business is synonymous with people. Business all starts with people and business all ends with people. So keep your relationships good: treat them more than fair, go the extra mile but don't be taken advantage of.

HEALTH

The old saying take care of your body, it's the only one you have. Now is the time to do healthy things in your

life. Eat healthy, exercise on a regular bases, quit
smoking, if you smoke, be careful with the alcohol. Get a
yearly physical; get you eyes checked once a year when
you are over 40. Men are at a high risk for heart disease
so watch what you are doing. Our health is something we
also take for granted; I have reached the age where I
notice how difficult it is to do some of the simple things I
used to do. So the sooner you start watching your health
the better off you will be, as you get older.

All my love,
Dad

Anonymous
Born 1946

A THOUGHT FROM THE DAD'S CORNER
"Health is not valued till sickness comes."
Dr. Thomas Fuller (1654 – 1734)

To my daughters Amber (29 years of age), Jennifer (25 years of age), and Sara (21 years of age),

Know that: I never expected to live in a house with little girls. I only had brothers. The thought of all little girls was foreign to me. But, with some prayer and practice I think God has allowed me to be a decent girls' dad. I adore all three of you. I have sometimes failed, but always tried to show all of you how important you are to me, and how you have defined who I have become today.

The top values that I encourage for you are:

THINK OF OTHERS
Treat others with the same patience and understanding you would like shown to you. Give the other guy a break. Try to put yourself in the shoes of the people you deal with. Don't expect anyone to show kindness back to you because you were kind. It just doesn't work that way. If others are kind to you, it's a bonus. Be kind for the sake of your own peace of mind.

MAKE GOOD CHOICES
I know you're tired of hearing me say that. But we become our choices; we are freed or imprisoned by the quality of the choices we make. Establish high principles to guide your decisions. Think long-term when making choices.

AVOID DEBT
I believe debt is a product financial institutions market and sell to people who don't know how to handle money. Borrowing to buy a home can be a good choice. But charging for something today that will be gone tomorrow is to be discouraged. Ask yourself if the purchase will outlast the payment plan. Charging a pizza that won't be paid off for two months just doesn't sound smart.

RESPECT TIME
Start a retirement fund as soon as possible and let it grow with time. Even if you need to stop contributing in a few years, the earlier you start, it will still keep working for you. This is an example of respecting time. Allow time to

be your partner and work for you. You will never find time; if you need time you will have to make it. Lost time can never be found. It's true; time does fly, so decide to be the pilot. Don't be afraid of doing something that may take years to finish. The years will pass anyway. Be willing to invest time in yourself.

THE FRONT PORCH TEST

Visualize yourself sitting on the front porch of a house on your 95th birthday. In your mind: who is in the front yard, who is on the porch with you, and who is sitting next to you? Now, ask yourself, "What and who would be important to me on that front porch; are my choices and actions today going to take me to that place?"

Love,
Dad

Ronald 'Ron' Dean Calhoun
1954
Northern Kentucky University
• Bachelor's Degree in Electronic Media & Video Production with a minor in journalism
• Bachelor's Degree in Public Relations with a sports entertainment marketing area of concentration
CAREER – Electronic Technician, Professional Magician, Public Relations Specialist, Videographer
HOBBIES – Magic enthusiast, Video Production

To my three children Tanya, Ian, and Angela (between the ages of 27 and 37),

Know that: I am extremely proud of you. Parenting is not easy; raising children is difficult. Nobody trains you how to be a parent. When you have your kids, you think you know everything, but in reality you don't. Parenting is difficult. Maybe I was lucky, but I am very, very proud of you.

The top values that I encourage for you are:
ALLOW YOUR CHILDREN TO SPEND TIME WITH THEIR GRANDPARENTS
One of the things that are very important when you are bringing up your kids is to allow them to interact with their grandparents. I see that now. I grew up without grandparents and I think that was something that was missing in my childhood. Grandparents are definitely a very positive influence. This influence makes kids more balanced loving people.
SPEND QUALITY TIME WITH YOUR OWN CHILDREN
Something I regret is that I have always worked twelve hours a day; that I didn't have enough time to devote to you. However, I always tried to give you my best available time. Quality family time has to be a high priority. Now that I have four grandchildren, I really think that I do appreciate the meaning of life more than when I had my own kids. When you have kids, you are just too young and too busy to appreciate them!
LIVE WITH INTENSITY
You can go through life experiencing events without really not fully engaging in anything. Let me explain: You need to have "intensity" in what you are doing. When you play sports, for example, you have to do your best to win. At one point in your life you have to develop that intensity and pass it to your children. Families and people that have intensity enjoy life and get involved in new activities, and they are more proactive and engaged in life.

HAVE A GOOD ATTITUDE
Attitude makes the difference. Two people may have the
same qualification but one can see a situation as a huge
problem, and the other person may see it as an
opportunity. How you look at things is important in life as
well as in business. If you take on marriage with a good
attitude, you can solve your problems. Marriage is not
always easy, but with the attitude that you will make it,
then you will. I have also tried to give you an optimistic
view of life. Pessimists will never develop anything or do
anything. To do anything and to enjoy life you have to
have an optimist's respect for life. I am happy that you
respect life and are very optimistic.

FOCUS YOUR ENERGY AND EFFORTS
You have to have a balanced life and be in control. This
sounds like a cliché, but in time, becomes important.
Some people are obsessed with things that are not that
important. Focus your energy on the things that are
really, really important. Make your effort count.

CHOOSE GOOD FRIENDS
When it comes to friends, you have to make good
judgments based on fairness and without prejudice, but
at the end of the day you may need to make difficult
decisions and eliminate some bad friendships.

All my love, Dad

NAME: Alfonso Cornejo
BIRTH YEAR: 1947
EDUCATION: Chemical Engineer,
University of Mexico
CAREER: Procter and Gamble;
Clorox Company; Chiquita;
President of Hispanic Chamber,
Cincinnati, USA.
HOBBIES: Magic-Collector

To my daughter Rose and sons Leo and Art (now deceased) between the ages of 58 and 65,

Know that: I am proud of you; you are good children. You have never been in any trouble at all, ever, and nowadays even some prominent and affluent families have children who get into trouble, doing things they shouldn't be doing. You both go to Church, as you should; you two have always done the right thing.

The top values that I encourage for you are:

FORM GOOD HABITS

Here is a story about what my dad told me. I had a great dad and he told me when I was about 9 or 10 that life is all about habits: Good habits and bad habits. It is very important. Think of a habit like a rope. For example, if you want to make a rope by hand, then you would start with one little strand, and it would probably be easy to break: a one year old could break the strand. But then you add another strand and so on. When you go up to the 5th or 6th strand it is still easy to break, but not as easy. Then you build the rope larger. Each day you add the strands it gets tougher and tougher to break. The same as habits: whether a good or a bad habit. And in about 80 or 90 days, you have enough strands of a rope— a habit—you just cannot break it. This is the way they are formed.   One of the things my dad told me was to do the right things. You both have good habits and do what you should do. And I want this, Leo and Rose, to be passed on to you.

BE GOD-CENTERED

It is a shame in this society that the Lord is neglected because He is just not important enough to them. People will travel 600 miles to see Elvis Presley's grave, but those same people can't drive 2 miles to go to church. And church, by far, is more important since your life should be built around Jesus. We are all going to die. Your body will die and decay, but your soul: that is the important thing; that will be around forever. A lot of people say they believe in God, but do they really believe in God? I don't think so. If they really believed in all the miracles that He turned water into wine and fed all those people, and all that He has done, then they would be breaking down the door to be as close to God as they can. Celebrities get more glory than Jesus Himself. Too often, God gets the leftovers. Ann and I say three rosaries a day, and we do pray together everyday.

GRATITUDE
Always be grateful. Every morning when I get up, the first thing I do is look at Jesus on the wall and I thank Jesus for every day I have. My wife and I--as active as we are, and as old as we are--are not on any medication. This is because it is a miracle of Jesus: this, we believe in our hearts. Always be grateful to people. If someone does something for you, don't ignore it. There are few things much worse than being ungrateful and taking the goodness of people for granted.

PUT NEGATIVES INTO PERSPECTIVE
One of my favorite sayings is: "From the day you are born and until you are in the hearse, nothing is never so bad that it couldn't be worse." There's never been a truer statement in this world. You name me anything that happens and it could always be worse. When Ann broke her wrist, instead of crying about it, one of the first things we said was, "thank you, Jesus"... that is wasn't her hip, that it wasn't her back... or worse.

Love, Dad!

	Art Dickerson Born: 1923 Married to Ann for 65 years Career: Fuller Brush – Field Manager Interest: Music – Singing - guitar

To my son Ray III of age 26, my stepdaughter Shelby of age 26, and my daughter Samantha of age 16,

Know that: Ray, I couldn't be prouder. You have come a long way in the fire service. If your son or daughter, or any family member, follows the dream that you have, and it makes life good for *them,* and they want to carry on that dream, then that is the highest honorable thing I could ever imagine. And I do that myself with my own dad. I want to be in construction with him on my days off. He enjoys it and I want to enjoy it with him. My daughters, you two are my dream. Shelby, you are a great person and I love you as if you are my own. Samantha, when you look at me with those blue eyes, then I just melt. I can get mad at you, but cannot stay mad for long, and Shelby, the same way. Ray, with your big brown eyes and dark hair.... I never really could get mad at any of you three kids to the point of anything beyond just raising my voice from time to time to get your attitudes in check.

The top values that I encourage for you are:
LIFE'S LESSONS
I learned a lot of life lessons from working with my dad in construction. He taught me to work hard, earn what you get, and appreciate what you have. Treat people the way you want to be treated. Give a man an honest day's work for an honest day's pay. So, be true to yourself. Enjoy your job. Always look for somebody to talk to—family, friends, coworkers. When times get tough, don't hold it in.
DO IT
Don't expect things to be given to you - you have to earn it. Respect isn't given to anybody. You have to earn the respect from your colleagues. Be true to yourself and honest and open. Do it like I would want you to do it. Do it proudly, do it honorably, do it respectfully. Just treat people like you want to be treated. I try to instill in you, my kids, the core values of working hard and living life to the fullest. Everyday is a new adventure. So, go out there and be positive and make a difference in your life, and

that difference that you make in *your* life will affect someone else out there, in one way or another.

BE AROUND GOOD PEOPLE

I always tell the guys around here that you are only as good as the people you have around you. If you want to be a leader or a spokesperson, then just step up and do the right thing, and look at who is around you. That is what will make you the better person. As parents, we look at our kids when they are young adults, and say, "Who are your friends?" Then we learn a lot about our kids by who their friends are. If you have good friends, solid-minded young individuals, then you have something to be proud of.

FAMILY

I have been fortunate and blessed to have good family and friends around me. I am proud of my family, my wife and kids, mom and dad, and brothers and sisters. Without them--who all gave me the opportunity to do what I needed to do--then I may not be here as I am today. I am fortunate, and I am blessed and I am happy. And I see my son following in my footsteps and I am proud and happy but, of course, I worry---because that's my son.

Love, Dad

Ray Dishman, Jr.
Born: 1967
Campbell County High School
Construction
Assistant Fire Chief of Central Campbell County Fire District
Hobbies: hunting, fishing, sports

To my daughter Becky and my two sons, Mark and David, who are between the ages of 45 and 48 years old,

Know that: we both love you. We hope that we have shown our love and concern for you throughout your lives. Know that I want your hearts to be open to God so that God may have His way because that will enrich your lives so much.

The top values that I encourage for you are:

UNDERSTAND THAT CHILDREN ARE INDIVIDUALS
As parents, know that there is no one pattern that will fit all children. Children are all different. What will work for one child will not necessarily work for another. When as parents, if you have more than one child, you have to approach each child differently and deal with them differently.

EXPRESS YOUR LOVE TO YOUR CHILDREN
We as parents need to tell our children that we love them. Don't just be scolding them and correcting them. I sometimes see in a store where the child steps out of line, and the parent goes out and slaps them. That is the wrong thing to do. You can correct them and take them to one side and get them to notice what is happening, without making such a big to-do out of it. General correction is by far the way to go.

SHARE YOUR FAITH
We all need to share with our children our faith in God, not lecturing to them, but just expressing how we came to know the Lord. Our children's experiences maybe slightly different but probably still have the same basis.

SHARE YOUR CHRISTIAN CONVERSION STORY
Frances and I came to know the Lord at different ages: she as a child mostly through her mother's influence, but the Spirit of God didn't speak to me until I was a teenager. My parents wanted me to join the church and I

did, one Easter Sunday. I had enough knowledge to answer all the questions correctly but I had no clue what I was doing. It wasn't until I started going to another little Methodist church that I was attending--, oh, I'd go to all the youth meetings, I'd go on Sundays, and Wednesday nights and attend all the activities. But then, one night, I went home from a service and somehow I was troubled in my heart. I did not feel Conviction, as we call it, at the service itself, yet, somehow God was speaking to me. I tried to bargain with God and give to Him certain areas of my life. Then, finally, I gave all I knew to give to God. His peace came into my heart and my life, and I accepted Jesus. And that was really the beginning of my Christian life. This Faith is something to share with our children. I do not always push for conversion; I tell my story and I want the other person to think, "Maybe this could happen to me." It may be slightly different for them but still it is God working in their hearts and minds. When I am working with children, as a clown or a magician, I tell them about how I don't know when God will speak to their hearts, but when He does, that is the time to say, "Yes" to Him and ask Him to enter their hearts and enter their lives. He wants to become your forever Friend, throughout your life--in childhood struggles, and as an adult---throughout life.

Love, Dad

John Dutill
Born in 1935
Married to Frances for 53 years
Education: Asbury College (near Lexington, KY)
Career: pastor for 20 years
Hobbies: collecting coins, magician and clown performances

To my son and daughter between the ages of age 34 and 43,

Know that: I love you very, very much and, like most parents, I want you both to be successful, to have responsibility and accountability. Fortunately or unfortunately, the path to getting there can sometimes be extremely difficult. But no matter what, I will never give up on you.

The top values that I encourage for you are:

GET RIGHT WITH GOD AND SET GOALS
To my daughter; I would like you to get right with God and I know that you have already started. I would like to see you set the example for your daughter, to get her more involved, and I know that with your scheduling and everything else, this can be difficult for you. I think once that relationship is established, other things will become a lot easier for you. I know it is difficult, but I am so proud of you and all that you have accomplished and there's still a lot of blessings yet to come to you. I think you have set a goal in your life and that you will not let the situation get out of hand again. I am so proud of you. Everything you are doing now is right. You are going down the right path but I would just like church and religion to become a little stronger in your life than what it is now. I think that would be a big plus.

TAKE FINANCIAL RESPONSIBILITY AND SET A GOOD EXAMPLE
To my son; I am equally as proud of you. However, there have been more disappointments – primarily because of the financial struggles. If they weren't an issue—then I think our relationship would be better because I wouldn't have sounded so negative over the years. That doesn't mean that I love you any less. I love you equally as much as your sister. However, you do need to get with a financial advisor or get some kind of financial help in order to take me out of the middle of the equation. Talk to somebody to try to get your life put back together. It

is obvious that I cannot do it. I have tried. As I have told your sister, I think you need to start coming to church and to get your kids involved. Since they have been there in the past, I think they would enjoy doing it again. As a parent you have to set the example and they learn by your leadership. You have to be the one to take the lead. You just can't put things off and live for today and let tomorrow take care of itself. You are important to them. There has to be some change that takes place, sooner rather than later. It is affecting everybody's life--- your life, your children's lives, my life, and your sister's life. You have to be accountable for your mistakes, and, hopefully, learn from your mistakes. And you have not been doing that. I hope for you nothing but success. I think I have helped you, especially financially, as much as I can. Emotionally, I am always there for you. I wish you had a better relationship with me and not just come around when you need something. I would like to be a more important factor in your life and not just a handout to you. I am concerned about how you will turn out and how you will plan your life, as you get older. I have tried so hard to take care of you guys. When I die maybe things will get a little bit better. I feel sure your sister will use her inheritance as investments and get her life more together. But I fear at the time of my death that you will probably squander whatever is left and you will be no better off than what you are right now, unless you change the way you do things.

I love you both so very much,
Dad

Anonymous
Born 1945

To my adult daughters - Jennifer, Tracy, and Carrie,

Know that: I am proud of you and the strong & loving individual persons you have each become. Also, I am certain that your grandparents would be very proud of you, too. I am painfully aware that I have not been a consistently great father, but I have always done my best to be there for you when you needed me most. I have appreciated our relationships across all stages of your lives, from your newborn days to your current adulthood. Below are a few thoughts for you to consider: some are based on things that worked for me, and some are lessons from my mistakes.

The top values that I encourage for you are:

KEEP GOD IN YOUR LIFE
Give Him some of your time, your thought, your treasure. Invest in eternity. It is worth it.

STAY CLOSE WITH FAMILY
Family members are the only ones who truly care about you, so treat them like your dearest friends, and keep in touch. Don't let minor issues interfere with your long-term relationships. Let them know that you love them.

MAKE GOOD FRIENDS
To have friends, you have to be a friend. Listen before responding. Show respect, empathy, appreciation and encouragement. Have a sense of humor. You never know when you're starting your next friendship. Get involved in volunteer activities, where those around you are thinking of others; it will rub off and you will be happier. People don't care how much you know as long as they know how much you care (E. Larry Moles).

BE TRUE TO YOURSELF
Make sound decisions based on your values. Seek others' opinions, but decide for yourself. Develop your cornerstone values for guidance: e.g., integrity, honesty, love, loyalty, charity, humility, tolerance, and commitment. Be content with yourself. Do things that you

enjoy and you will be good at them. Life is not a matter of milestones, but of moments (Rose Kennedy).

BALANCE WORK AND LIFE, SPENDING AND SAVING
Good things happen when you work hard. Your grandpas and your uncles are good examples. But I suggest working to live, not living to work. Find the right balance for your own happiness.

You are better off than 80+% of the world population; appreciate that instead of wishing for the upper 20%. Life can be enjoyable without the best this or latest that.

Think about your happiest memories, and they probably won't be about "things". Live within your budget, and go ahead and buy the things that are truly important. Save the rest; you will need it for colleges and retirement.

My wish for you is a life filled with happiness. I love you,

Dad

Gerry Ellspermann, Born 1952 Evansville Mater Dei Catholic High School (Honor Society, student government leader, basketball, baseball, cross country) Purdue University: BS – Industrial Management (Finance) – With honors	Occasionally a mover Occasionally a repairman Occasionally a financier Occasionally a sense of humor Mostly simple Always loyal
Procter & Gamble/J M Smucker - 30 years Habitat for Humanity Executive Director - 3 years	
Volunteerism – at least 5,000 hours - Youth sports coach - Church outreach - Habitat for Humanity - Project leader on 15 homes thru 2011 - Two mission trips thru early 2012	
Son, brother, friend, husband, father, co-worker, volunteer	

To my daughter Paula and to my Son Michael between the ages of age 43 and 46,

Know that: This is being written at a point in your lives where you have practiced and demonstrated superbly the below listed qualities as well as many others not mentioned. You have experienced joy and overcome some of life's painful lessons. Through it all your accomplishments have been great and many. You have become responsible, contributing, adults of high moral character and integrity. I am extremely proud and blessed that you are my children.

The top values I encourage for you are:
PERSISTENCE & DETERMINATION
When you get knocked down you get back up and go at it again. Life will always present you with good times and bad times, easy decisions and tough ones. Decisions have consequences. Pray to the Lord for guidance before making some of your more difficult decisions. Think hard and pray about what you are about to commit to. Plan good plans and follow up on them. Those who achieve meaningful success and accomplishments in this world do so through hard work and perseverance.
LIVE WITH JOY
When you wake up each morning try not to dwell on all of the things that are problems, or perceived problems in your life. Emphasize the good things and look for the joy in living. Being positive and looking for the good in life makes it all worthwhile. Life is meant to be enjoyed not merely endured. Practice at being happy!!! Make your countenance reflect a strong internal positive attitude. Being a person who is always unhappy, complaining and disagreeable projects a negative image. Life is a wonderful gift. Work and strive to be joyful and live it to the fullest.
BE PROUD TO BE AN AMERICAN
Be grateful and thank God that you were born an American. Generations of Americans have served and died to preserve our freedom. Do not take our liberties

for granted. Those who have experienced tyranny, suppression, socialism, dictatorship(s) and have subsequently achieved American citizenship treasure their newfound freedom. Most Americans who are citizens by birth have no clue as to how blessed they are and do not appreciate what they have. Fulfill your responsibilities as citizens, instill patriotic values in you children and do not allow people to denigrate the United States of America. The preservation of our liberty requires eternal vigilance.

LOOK AT LIFE WITH A LONG TERM PERSPECTIVE

When my father died at the relatively young age of 62 I vowed to try and live my life to the fullest. Now 40 years later I am at a completely different vantage point. Mortality at this age is a lot more real with each passing year. A great deal of whom we are and how we live is the result of what we have been taught and how we have been raised. Look at life from a multi-generational standpoint. Use experiences from your grandparents, your parents, your children, and some day your grandchildren to enrich and deepen the meaning of your lives. All these stages in our lives are God's design, relish them and do not rush through them. Life is a continuum, as you have more experiences, and mature, things looked at from a longer perspective make more sense.

With All my Love,
Dad

Bill Enghauser   Born 1942
Married to Odette for 19 years
1964 - AS, Electronics Technology Ohio College of Applied Science
1974 - BS, Business Administration /Computer Science, Ohio State University
1979 - MS, Computer Systems and Operations Research, Purdue University
CAREER - Systems Analyst/Programmer, Manager Telecommunications Industry
HOBBIES – Automotive Restoration, Aircraft, Reading, Travel

To my wonderful sons, Paul of age 45 and Peter of age 41,

Know that: you two are my pride and joy. We laughed and cried through good times and bad. As children, I soothed your aches and pains, consoled you on your mistakes, praised you on your awards. You two fought the good fight and are still ahead of the game. I am proud of you. Keep up the good work.

Well, guys, as you know, I am at the ripe old age of eighty years young, still standing, bright-eyed and bushy-tailed. So at this stage, I thought I would reminisce with you about the past and speak of the present.

The top values that I encourage for you are:

THE FUTURE
Don't worry about the things you cannot change in the future: they will take care of themselves, one-way or the other.

EDUCATION
Remember when you were kids in school during your formative years? I told you to get the best out of your lessons. Ask the teacher questions if you don't understand. Don't ask your classmates. They don't know any more about the problem than you do.

GOOD JUDGMENT
Depend on your own intuition and good judgment. You both chose skilled trades that will carry you through to the rest of your working careers.

POSITIVE ATTITUDES
Life is what you make of it. You can smell the roses of life or stand knee-deep in a field of weeds. Enjoy life. Life can truly be a bowl of cherries, if you cultivate good friends and companions who know how to laugh at the world and have a good sense of humor.

On the downside, life can be a bunch of sour grapes if you listen to those who are always the gloom and doom type. Avoid them at all cost.

GOALS
Set your course for a brighter future as best as you are capable---because on a clear day...you can see into eternity.

Peaches 'n' Cream,
Love, Dad

Paul Ernst
Born 1931
Married to Gisela for 48 Years
Purcell High School
New York Technical Institute
Certified – Electronics
American Tool Company
Signode Corp.
Hobbies and interest:
History, Reading, Sumi-E Painting,
Art of Magic and Illusions, Para Normal,
Glass Enameling and Bead Making, Wood Carving,

A THOUGHT FROM THE DAD'S CORNER
"I am still determined to be cheerful and happy, in whatever situation I may be; for I have also learned from experience that the greater part of our happiness or misery depends upon our dispositions, and not upon our circumstances."
Martha Washington (1732 - 1802)

To my daughter Jessica of age 27,

Know that: I am a better person because of you. I have a fuller life because of you. I get to see all of your mother's good traits in you---whom I love so much--- and that is a wonderful thing. I have learned a lot by watching the way you have lived your life. You have an intention of doing something and then you do it. It is a wonderful thing to see. You do something because you don't think that you can't do it. It never crosses your mind that you couldn't have hiked up the whole Appalachian Trail. You said, "I am going to do it. I am going to be a doctor" and you did. "I am going to hike the whole Appalachian Trail" and you did. "We are going to climb Mt. Whitney, the highest mountain in the United States, you and me" and we did. These are things I never would have done, but you roped me into doing them with you. And I'm so glad I did.

The top values that I encourage for you are:

RESPECTING MONEY
Live slightly below your means. Don't spend too much and don't save too much. Find a good balance.

HAVING FUN
The main thing is to have lots of love everyday and lots of fun. Life is too short.

CHOOSING FRIENDS
You become what you are around. That can be good or bad, so choose your friends carefully because it can be good or bad what you are around.

BEING NICE
It is good to be a good person but it is nicer to be nice. I know it sounds like a cliché—good to be good, but nicer to be nice, but love goes a long way: spread the love and share the love.

CONTINUE ENLIGHTENING OTHERS

Most people who are around you, Jessie, feel like they have come away a better person because of your kindness, the way you share your love, your values, and your outlook on life. I have heard this from several people including your teachers and professors. And I feel the same way, too.

Love, Dad

P.S. – Don't forget to check your oil.

	Doug Gehner Born: 1950 Education: Western Hills High School, University of Cincinnati Musician/Entertainer/ Farmer

A THOUGHT FROM THE DAD'S CORNER
"You can make more friends in two months by becoming interested in other people than you can in two years by trying to get other people interested in you."   **Dale Carnegie**

To my son and two daughters, Ryan, Amanda, and Claire, who are between the ages of 6 and 28 years old,

Know that: you are each a gift from God and you have given me a life of fulfillment, joy and happiness.

The top values that I encourage for you are:

FAITH IN GOD
I encourage for you a deep, intimate, and abiding faith in God. All that you are is wrapped up in my relationship with God. I truly view you as blessings that God has given me to be a steward over. Because of that, I love you, I cherish you, and I nourish you. I try to teach you both by word and example. And I hope that I am delivering you to Him for His glory. I know that sounds overly preachy, but at the end of the day, that is my hope. If I accomplish that as a father with you, then I have hit my ultimate highest target.

LOYALTY AND DEVOTION
I encourage loyalty and devotion to family.

LEADERSHIP
I encourage you to be leaders and independent thinkers and self-confident adults.

GETTING THE MOST OUT OF LIFE
Beyond a shadow of a doubt, for me personally, and I hope a view that you kids will adopt, is that you get the most out of life by what you give to other people. Giving is not always defined in dollars and cents. Sometimes it is a listening ear or a compassionate heart or some words of encouragement or taking somebody on an errand that they, otherwise, could not run without your help. It is doing something to make somebody else's life valuable. I encourage everyone, but surely you, my kids, to think in terms of when you lend something to somebody, don't lend it, but give it as a gift, and then encourage the

recipient of the gift to pass that gift forward to somebody else.

GOOD WORK ETHIC

I try to model for you a good, solid, energetic work ethic, but what is most important to me is that you see my passion for whatever work I choose to do. Whatever you pursue in life, whether it be something that I would have chosen for you, or something that you have chosen, even if it seems to come out of left field, it needs to be something about with, and for with, you feel a lot of passion. At the end of the day your work has to nourish and fulfill you in some very critical ways. It is a third of your life. You will spend one-third of your life working. And, consequently, that third of your life needs to be fulfilling and productive, and if it is not, then you need to find what is fulfilling and productive.

Love, Dad

Clyde Gray
Born: 1955
Married to Kalena for 12 years
Education: Wake Forest University, NC
   (Major - Speech Communications and Theater Arts)
Career: News Broadcaster for WCPO TV Cincinnati, OH
Hobbies: Golf, Reading, Writing

To my two magnificent daughters of age 28 and 30,

Know that: you have brought so much joy into my life and I have treasured every moment. OK, not every moment was easy by any means – but for the most part you were just doing your job: fighting to grow up – to grow independent – to become who you were meant to be – strong, loving and beautiful daughters.

The top values that I encourage for you are: There are so many things to share but I'd like to focus on relationships.

10 COMMANDMENTS OF A POSITIVE RELATIONSHIP

Honesty - No positive relationship (absolutely none) can or will survive without honesty – always be honest with each other.

Love – is an emotion – Emotions are a result of how we interpret the world around us. Emotions come and go: one minute you may be happy – the next minute you may be sad; one moment you may be in a loving mood – the next moment maybe not so much. We have no lock to keep in the good emotions and no door to keep out the bad ones. So, nurture positive emotions -

Kindness – be kind to each other even when you don't feel like it -

Appreciation - Be thankful – Appreciate even the simplest of things -

Respect – Respect each other - Even when you disagree – especially when you disagree -

Boundaries – understand them well – for example – married people have different boundaries than single people: a good reason for married people not to hang out excessively with single people. Boundaries are usually invisible and not always easy to determine – the fewer times you cross the boundaries the fewer times you will be saying that you are sorry – The boundaries in each relationship are different.

Control – don't control the other nor be controlled by the other -

Dignity – keep dignity in yourself and in each other –
protect each other's dignity.
Sense of Humor – lighten up – let some of the small
things slide: chances are – you're wrong about it anyway
– I hope you are strong enough to laugh at yourself.
Practice - Live these commandments – For example -
Dieting is not complex: the main ingredient is discipline.
We may know the rules of a diet – but the weight doesn't
come off until we apply those rules – and continue to
apply those rules to keep the weight off – it's a way of
living. So is it with these rules of a positive relationship.
To know them is good. But they will not bring you a good
happy relationship until you live them.

When your relationship is not working – review these
rules – chances are – if you're honest with yourself –
you'll find one or more of these rules have been broken.

All my love,
Dad

Anonymous
Born 1953

To my beloved son Troy and his wife Kristin, my middle daughter Tracy and her husband Mike, my baby daughter Trisha and her husband Seth, and all of my grandchildren, Jared, Jordan, Taylor, Cooper, Joel, Jonah, Micah, and Chloe – each of you are the joy and happiness of my life.

Know that: your Mom and I have often said to one another, "God has truly blessed us beyond measure when He allowed us to be your parents, in-laws, and grandparents. Each of you is truly a gift from God that is loved and cherished deep within our hearts and spirits.

The top values that I desire and encourage for your lives can be remembered by the following acrostic - L-A-U-G-H. Learn how to L-A-U-G-H and you will be complete, happy, and successful.

L – Love God with all your heart! This is the key to true joy, happiness and fulfillment. Nothing in life can give this to you except God, Himself. The Bible tells us, "For where your treasure is, there your heart will be also" (Matthew 6:21). Treasure (love) God with all your heart and you will have true joy, happiness, and your life will be successful.

A – Accept each day as a gift from God! Face each day with strength, confidence, and power knowing your love for God and that each day is a gift from Him to you. Accept whatever comes to you during the day as a means for God to build His character in your life.

U – Use the gifts and abilities God has given you to better the world you live in. Each of you has been given special gifts, talents and abilities by God. Use them to serve Him faithfully and to better the world in which you live. Each of you has been blessed so be a blessing to others in Jesus' Name.

G – Glorify God in your life! Allow His godly character to be developed in your life so that it will bring glory and honor to Him. The Apostle Paul states, "But the fruit of the Spirit is love, joy, peace, patience, kindness, goodness, faithfulness, gentleness and self-control..." (Galatians 5:22-23). Allow these character qualities to be developed in your life and your life will glorify God.

H – Help others to experience the love of God in Christ Jesus! The greatest contribution that you can make in life is helping others come to know Jesus Christ, God's Son, as their personal Savior. Other contributions are good but this one affects a person's eternity. Live each day with the passion to help others come to know Jesus as their Savior.

I am blessed to be your Father, Father-in-law, and Grandfather. Learn to L-A-U-G-H!

Love, Dad

Ben H. Hahn
Born 1950
Married to Brenda (42 Years)
Springfield High School, Battle Creek, Michigan
Asbury College – BA in Biblical Studies
Asbury Theological Seminary – Master of Divinity (90 hour Degree)
Asbury Theological Seminary – Doctor of Ministry Degree
Hobbies and Interest: Grandchildren, Hunting, Golfing, Family Activities

To my two sons, Travis of age 39 and Todd of age 36, and my four grandchildren (whom we are raising),

Know that: I love you very much. As our adopted sons, the fact that you are adopted makes no difference. Biological or not, "you are my boys" and I am very proud of what you have accomplished and what you have to look forward to in life.

The top values that I encourage for you are:

FOLLOW THE GOLDEN RULE
I want you to live by the Golden Rule: treat others, just as you would want to be treated yourself.

GIVE KINDNESS
Be kind to other people and to each other. If you overwhelm someone with your kindness then it really melts him or her down. I found this out in life, and it certainly carries over into business. Just overwhelm a person with kindness and it goes a long way. I am not taking a hard line or anything, but some people don't seem to be able to be kind; they just don't know how to do that.

BE RESPECTFUL
Respect other people and respect other people's property. The key is you must first respect yourself. You have to have that self-respect and then the others will come naturally. If you don't respect yourself, then you don't have a chance of getting through life well.

MAKE GOOD CHOICES
You have to make good choices and they determine the outcome and the caliber of life that you will have. Before I'd get into something, I would always say to myself, "Would Mom be proud of what I am doing?" or "Do my parents have to live with the results of what I am doing?" I respected my parents dearly and there was that loving bond between us. You have to think of those things.

BE RESPONSIBLE

You must be responsible for what you do because you are going to endure the consequences, good or bad. You have to give back to the community. I try to exemplify that. I do a lot of speaking and fundraisers for charities because I know I need to give back

PUT GOD INTO YOUR LIFE

You definitely need God in your life. He controls everything if you just put Him in charge. A few years ago--when your mother, and then our little granddaughter, were dealing with a lot of serious health issues--during those hard times, I got really mad at God; I got angry. But I realize now, that through all of this, God helped me become stronger. We all go through stages of good and bad in life. Life is like a jump rope: it goes up and down. I realized that I could just sit there and cry about it, or I could get out and do something. Through this, my faith became stronger. So I go out there and I give more help to charitable organizations, to help people who needed support.

Love, Dad

Ed Hartman
Born: 1942
Married to Betty Jo for 45 years
Education: North Dearborn High
School - Miami University
Career: US Air Force,
Furniture Business over 40 years
Hobbies: Golf, Anti-bullying program
director; Charity fundraiser chairman

To my sons Robert (age 28) and Chris (age 25),

Know that: fathering is full time: Even till death.
Know that: I love you both.
Know that: both of you have grown to be fine men.
Know that: both of you will leave a Legacy.
Know that: it is ok to ponder, dabble, and conjecture.

The top values that I encourage for you are:

PRACTICE THE GREATEST COMMANDMENTS
Love God with all your heart, soul, mind and body.
Love thy neighbor as thy self. Or said a different way - Do
to others as you would have them do to you.

GENEALOGY
Understand your biological paternal & maternal roots:
Even past generations.
Carry on family traditions or start some of your own.
For example "Don't say I can't or Begin Middle Names
with the letter A or Do your best at what you do".
These traditions were passed on to me by my dad and his
dad to him.

BE WHO YOU ARE
Try not to be someone else unless you are acting. Acting
to be your self is best (good is not acceptable). Be your
best.
Be true to yourself. You will know when you're not.
Be true to others. They will know when you're not.
Be an optimist.
Think what the alterative to Alzheimer's is.
Don't be afraid to cry. Laughter usually follows.

INVEST IN

Time: God created time on the first day. When will be the
last day? Use it wisely, it goes by fast.

Education: There is a dictionary for all words,
everything under and above the sun. Learn all you can.
To be smart - learn what you don't know. Problems have
many solutions. Many solutions have problems.
People: Get to know them. Remember - learn what you
don't know. Let them get to know you. They're lost if they
don't.
Money: Get debt free. Not everything costs money.
Spend within your means. It's not about how much you
make.

With Love,
Dad

Patrick Hartzel
Born: 1955
Courter Tech High School
Cincinnati State
Vending Tech
All Star Vending
Councilmen
   North College Hill
Ward Chairman
Precinct Executive
Genealogist
Magician

A THOUGHT FROM THE DAD'S CORNER
"He that is of the opinion money will do everything may well be suspected of doing everything for money." **_Benjamin Franklin (1706 – 1790)_**

To my youngest Son age 37 and my deceased Son,

Know that: I love the heck out of both of you. You
probably did not think that I did all the time, but I did.
You cannot always get along 100% of the time, because if
one person has to be the father, and wants to share his
knowledge with you, then sometimes you just don't really
want to hear that. I was not very successful with my
oldest Son. My youngest Son, you were exposed to a lot
of things that you shouldn't have been - because of your
older brother - which I think really helped you a lot. I
was a single father from the time you were fourteen and
six. You and I have a very close relationship. We
probably speak several times a week, and we have
Sunday dinners together every Sunday. You love to eat
and I love to cook, so it works out very well for both of
us.

To my deceased Son: You were lost to me because of
drugs. You had a wife and two beautiful kids, but,
unfortunately, you threw all that away. Your loss was a
total waste of humanity. It breaks my heart; it rips my
heart out. If I could talk to you again, I would wish that
you would listen to me in terms of choosing your friends.
You were a very smart young man and had a lot of good
things going for you. And you just really went down the
wrong path.

To my youngest Son, the best I can say is that I have
been a very good bad-example. Everything I do, you
chose not to do and it has worked out very, very well for
you. You are my rock. And I am very proud of you.

The top values that I encourage for you are:

STAY ON A GOOD PATH
For my youngest Son, you should just stay the course.
You have done a beautiful job with your life so far. You
are a very creative person and you work well with your
kids as a teacher and sometimes in different ways than a

lot of teachers do. You are a heck of a human being, and I am very, very proud of you.

GOOD DECISIONS

In terms of decisions, you and I had a conversation one time when I was feeling really bad about the loss of your brother. You said, "Dad, I had to make the same decisions as he did and I chose to make different decisions." That conversation was about eight years ago. To this day that statement remains in my mind.

GIVING BACK

What came out of this tragedy is that my goal now is to work with young children to keep them from making wrong decisions. I am working on a program now where I bring in my best friend, my dog Buddy, to point out the importance of choosing your friends. The next meeting I would bring in animals from the shelter. We would play with them and show the kids that with every pleasure in life there is responsibility with it. In the room that we are doing this in, there will be duct tape on the floor. The tape goes in a straight line and it then goes to the right and goes to the left. We will then talk how we make choices in our life. Hopefully, if the shelter will allow it, we will be able to take the kids there and show them that for every joy you get in life, there is also a responsibility. After seeing where the animals live we'll have the kids clean cages---and, of course, those cages look remarkably like a jail. I hope to make the point, that you do not want to take the wrong turn, but that you do have choices in life.

Love, Dad

	Harry Himebaugh Born: 1942 Education: Louisville Country Day and University of Louisville (Psychology) Careers: Insurance and Realty Hobbies: Finding forever homes for dogs

To Jordan, Alexa, Quinnton, and Diana, who are between the ages of 13 and 17,

Know that: I love you dearly. I am proud of each and every one of you for different reasons. You are each such individuals; one is not like the other. I love each of you for your own special reasons. I am not always the greatest parent, and I have made mistakes, but I want you to understand that regardless of what I say or do, you are always most important to me.

The top values that I encourage for you are:

FAMILY
I want you to care more about people than things: than anything—care especially for family and especially each other. Take care of yourself; take care of your family and love them more than you love yourself. If you take care of them, then they will take care of you. I want you four to always look after each other.

SERENITY PRAYER
In terms of the future, it is a cliché but do not worry about what is outside of your control. Don't worry about the things you cannot change tomorrow. Take care of yourself and learn, and tomorrow will take care of itself.

EDUCATION
You are at the age now where school and the teachers are there to teach you, and now it is your responsibility to take on the job of learning for yourself. You need to seek it out. Don't expect the people to be there to give it to you. You have to go out and get it, and make it for yourself, constantly doing that for yourself. Here I am, your father, at 45 years of age and I realize now, more than I did when I was your age, that everything my whole life has been about learning more, seeking more, learning something new to get through the situations.

POSITIVE ATTITUDE
Just always be positive and that will carry you through the times that are not so good.

CAREER
My whole life, my career, has always been, in a way, for service, and not a job for profit. I like my job. Whatever you choose to do, choose something that fulfills you. My job is something that I will never get rich doing and I know that it would make life more comfortable for you if it were. I know that you guys have had to sacrifice, probably more than I have, because I wasn't always there for birthdays and Christmases. But remember that I love you so much and my job was a way of taking care of you. And it was important for that reason.

Like I said in the beginning, be good to people and, that way, you will always feel good about yourself.

Love, Dad

Samuel Hodge
Born: 1966
Education: Northern Kentucky University
Married to Inna for 9 years
Police Officer, Highland Heights, KY
Military Reservist
Hobbies: Motorcycling, History

To my energetic son of age 4 and charming daughter of age 2,

Know that: I love you more than life itself. I am proud to serve my country and hope to keep it a safe place for you to grow up in. I hope that soon I will be able to spend more time with you but in the mean time please know that I think of you every single day.

The top values that I encourage for you are:

I'm going to keep this real basic – hopefully I'm there to teach you the rest about life but if for some reason I'm not, remember that I will always be with you in your heart. So here are the most important- hard- fact lessons I can leave with you.

Dos
Love God, love your country, and love your family.

Get a good education: A strong education; the best you possibly can.

Choose your spouse extremely carefully – don't rush into marriage – your spouse, whether you remain married or not, will most likely be an influence, positively or negatively, for as long as you live.

Be around good people.

DON'Ts
Don't do any illegal drugs – or even cigarettes. Enough said!

Keep alcohol to a minimum. It can and will sneak up on you. Too much will eventually destroy the things you cherish.

Don't get pregnant before the time is right. Children are for a lifetime.

Never spend any more time, than you absolutely have to,
around bad people.

Everything else will take care of itself.

All my love,
Dad

 Anonymous
Born 1978

A THOUGHT FROM THE DAD'S CORNER
"Let every nation know, whether it wishes us well or ill, that we shall pay any price, bear any burden, meet any hardship, support any friend, oppose any foe to assure the survival and the success of liberty." **John F. Kennedy (1917 – 1963), Inaugural address, January 20, 1961**

To my sons Steve of age 37 and Matthew of age 40, and my grandson Logan of age 15, whom we are raising,

Know that: I love all of you so much. I hope my advice was useful even though you did not think so as a teen. Logan, we love raising you. As difficult as it is being a teenager today, we are proud of you, for you navigate this part so very well. All of our grandchildren are so special.

The top values that I encourage for you are:

BE A GOOD LISTENER
By being a good listener, you will establish a great relationship with your spouse and your children and other important people in your life. I could use some improvement on this issue as well.

WATCH THE COMPANY YOU KEEP
Get the right people in your life and keep the wrong people out. Logan, for example, is very choosey about his friends—nothing to do with money or anything like that—but with character. He is a good judge of character. I think I did okay in that regard 50 years ago --ancient history-- but that is very good advice. Sometimes, people seem to go down the wrong path with the wrong people.

DON'T ACCEPT MEDIOCRITY
I remember I was in a ROTC summer camp in 1967, and in a training platoon out of 50 people, I turned out to be number 35. I thought, "Wow, I thought I was better than that!" Not that I figured I'd be in the top 10, but I might at least have been number 20. I don't want to be number 35 out of 50! Don't just get by, but try to do a better job.

PASSION
Have passion for what you do, or find another career. When you see people going through the motions, you think, "Oh, my gosh, what a boring day!" I am self-employed and I enjoy this, and I have passion for this. I have run into too many people who don't have passion for what they do, and it must make for a miserable life.

KNOW YOUR GIFTS
Know your gifts when you are young- if this is possible.
Then you will be prepared for your career by taking
appropriate courses. I have been with a church group that
did an interesting exercise of find "Your Gifts". I think
that schools should of course, go through such exercises:
So you would know if you are a people-person, an
extravert, an introvert and so on. I have come to
recognize that some people are late bloomers and do not
have a clue of their gifts as a teen. Your mother,
probably the most gifted person I know, did not know of
her extraordinary gifts until her thirties.

BE SINCERE
The world sees through a superficial person very quickly.
I think I can. I don't try to judge people, but if someone
strikes me as superficial, that is not a good place to start.
So be sincere in everything.

MAKE YOUR VALUES KNOWN
Make sure your kids know what you believe in, not that
you are going to make them believe it, but don't be
surprised if they do. Make the case for what you believe,
spiritually, and a whole lot of other things. Set a good
example. If you claim to believe something but then your
example is bad, they are not going to buy into that or
believe anything.

Love, Dad

Dallas Horn   Born 1944
Bachelors of Science – Electrical
Engineer – University of Cincinnati
MBA – University of Cincinnati
Certified Financial Planner
Married to Carol for 45 years
Career: Cin. Bell Telephone Co. -
    Product Manager -
    Economic Analyst
    Personal Communications Mgr
Christopher Financial
    Financial Services / Advisor
Hobbies and interest: Reading,
    jogging, biking, church activities

To my three daughters, Andrea, Colleen, and Bernadette, between the ages of 27 and 32,

Know that: Your births had to be more important than even our wedding day. It was always exciting driving down to St Mike's before delivery, and narrowing down the names, if you were a boy or a girl. They were all tough births, caesarians, and in those days, 10 days of rest and care before discharging you, 10 days! On the last trip home with Bernadette as an infant, your Granddad Patrick on the same day was going home to recover from another heart attack, and he lasted 11 months. It was natural to have a new life arriving, while another was naturally preparing for death. I didn't get to meet Mom's father, George, as he died about three years before we met.

The top values that I encourage for you are:

TRAVELS Since Mom was from Cincinnati, that was a big trip, at least twice a year in the early years when Grammy was still alive. We went off from there...Florida, the Atlantic Coast, Washington DC, Boston, New York... and later Britain, Europe, Ireland, Spain, more Florida, and California Disney.

EDUCATION and CAREERS I enjoy being a life-long learner and hope in your busy lives, you will always be keen on exploring new things. In some ways, I regret I did not study more or shoot for a doctorate. Regardless, I hope all three of you become life-long learners. In terms of your careers, always have plan A and B, and maybe C, as this economy is strange, and you never know what economic surprises await us.

FAITH AND FAMILY Now, as you are adults, we have had weddings and births, baptisms, and vacations together. You have both become great parents, and Bern has a role now as aunt who is there for both of you...babysitting, giving you sanity time. We are so proud of your raising of Owen, Hannah, and Conner.

MAGNANIMITY I always was taken with the word, *magnanimity*...a greatness of soul or spirit. It came from a professor I had at Fordham University. I tried to live it in our lives, and in my education career, treating people with a greatness of soul.

INTEGRITY I remember going up to the counter to buy tickets at Disney, and Andrea was with me. She had just passed the age (9) when she became an adult for purposes of Disney admission. I felt I could not lie, because, one's integrity is all you have. We fail enough, but this was one time when I could not fudge it for a few dollars.

YOUR ROLE MODEL---YOUR MOM Finally, I can't finish without talking about your Mom. We met in the most unusual circumstances in St Louis U, and the rest is history. Little did I know we would fall in love, marry, and have you three girls. She is the most generous person I know: today baking food for the Out of the Cold Program, giving blood yesterday, leading her RCIA program with all the busy details, phone calls, counseling, making hard decisions and keeping up on the latest practices, as well as bringing soup and extra food to some poor people who are lost without her as an anchor. I hope that you see in her a woman of faith and your role model for life and generosity.

Love, Dad

NAME: Paul M. Howard
BIRTH: 1941: Ottawa, Ontario, Canada.
(Father :Diplomat to Washington, New Orleans, and Brussels)
EDUCATION: St Patrick's College HS Ottawa; Gonzaga College HS Washington DC; De La Salle HS of New Orleans.
BA: St Patrick's College, Ottawa; BTh: St Paul University, Ottawa; MEd: University of Toronto.
CAREERS: High school teacher, Vice-Principal, Principal, Governmental relations officer; Legal and Financial Matters for Teachers' Associations
HOBBIES: Apple Computers, teaching Scripture to Adults, history, reading, genealogy, travel, fitness.

To my son and two daughters, Jarod, Jorden, and Erin, who are 32,29 and 26 years old respectively,

Know that: I love you very much. Your mother and I have always been a part of your lives on a daily basis. I have been very involved with each of you personally and that has been a desire of mine to this day. Erin, when you were away at school for a few years - that was always hard, but then you came back into our lives. Now that you are married and live back at home; that is very pleasing and something I have looked forward to. I have always tried to support each of you in whatever you did.

The top values that I encourage for you are:

FAMILY
An area I want to pass on to you kids is probably a philosophy I have always had, and that is for however many children that you have, you should love each one of them unconditionally and spend as much quality time as you can with them. I see with a lot of parents, especially in the field that I am in with childcare, and the parents are sometimes distant from their children, and I can see the effects it has on young children. I have always tried to be a vital part in your lives and to spend as much quality time with you as possible. There have probably been a lot of things in the business field that I could have done throughout the years, but that just wasn't where my heart was. My heart was in the family. You know how much we have been involved in our families, how much your Mammal and Papal were in our lives. That is a family value worth pursuing. Family has always been an important part of us.

CAREER
Business-wise, you all have tended to follow the same areas of interest that your mother and I have followed, and you all have gotten into the social service areas of work. I applaud you for that. I commend you for that. I think that has to be a calling from God because it takes a

special person to do those things and to be able to get up everyday with a smile on your face.

CHURCH

Another area that is important to me is the role that the Church has in your lives. I know you all have been brought up in the Church and have attended Church on a weekly basis with your family. Your mother and I continue to go to Church and it is my wish that you all will find churches that will become a vital part of your life and that you can get involved in and go to Church on a weekly basis to hear the preaching of the Lord and determine what that means in your lives. I am concerned with the generations today because they seem to be falling away from the Church, and so I look at each one of you and I wish that you would make the Church a more important part of your lives - even more than it is right now.

Love, Dad

George Kees III
Born: 1956
Education: Campbell County High School and Northern Kentucky University - Degree in Business
Married to Bonnie for 32 years
Career: Owner of Basic Trust Child Development Center
Real Estate investments, (previously medical device business)
Hobbies: golf; previously baseball and football coach

To my three amazing and wonderful sons Todd, Jason and Michael - between the ages of 30 and 40 years old,

Know that: I think about you many times every day. I love you more than you can ever know. I am very proud of each one of you. Each of you is very different from one another, which makes you three even more special to me. One thing that you do have in common is you are good men and are very caring people. This is an opportunity to pass on to you, my sons, some ideas that I have strong feelings about in your lives.

The top values that I encourage for you are:
FAMILY
The most important thing to me, next to GOD is our family. These are the people that love you and want the best for you. It is important to keep these relationships alive and well. Too often we get busy and lose contact with each other. We all need to make an extra effort to call Mom, or Dad, or your brothers, to tell them what you are doing, or ask them if they are ok, or do they need anything, or, *"Hey, I just called to say 'I love you'."* I know people that don't even know where their family is. I never want to let us slip away from each other. The three of you stay close, especially when Mom and Dad are no longer here.
SELF IMPROVEMENT
Education is a great place to start. Even if you have your Bachelors degree or whatever education level you have, we should all be trying to improve ourselves every day. In this day and age people that stand still get left behind. My favorite team is the Patriots because everyday they are taught, to improve every day. Tom Brady, as good as he is, he works as hard as anybody or harder. That's how he got where he is today. You don't have to be Tom Brady; be yourself, but be as good as you can be. You don't want to have regrets later---*if only I had done these things*. Examples of what some of these things could be: take one course each year, something you like; learn a second language; take a cooking class if you like to eat; study for

a new career--- you never know when the job you have is no longer needed. Don't let the present control your future: you take control. You have the power to control what happens to you by planning ahead. This does take some work, but anything worthwhile, does. You will thank yourself later for the effort.

FINANCIAL

Financial security is about planning, patience, and discipline. Live below your means. Don't spend more money than you make. Spend less so you can save for the future and things you need now. Don't use credit cards as a loan. Use them in an emergency or as a convenience. _Always pay them off each month._ Never carry a balance---it will eat you up.

When you get a raise, increase your 401K Deduction by 1 % each time. You won't miss it, but it will get you where you want to be when it's time to stop working. This is the type of plan we followed; it worked very well for us. If you don't have the cash to buy something, save until you do. Once you have a good savings, you have breathing room to do the things you want. Some of these things you are probably already doing, but I am just reiterating because they are important.

Do what's right in your heart. Treat people how you want to be treated. Most importantly, have fun along the way and you can't go wrong.

Your best friend,
Love, Dad

Charles (Chuck) Ketterer   Born 1946
Married to Barbara for 43 years
Newport Catholic High School
University of Cincinnati:
Associates in Mechanical Engineering
Manufacturing Engineering 38 years
Hobbies and interest: Violin, Bonsai, Skiing, Golf, Bowling, World Champion Horseshoe Pitcher, Wine Making and Vineyard, Weight Lifting, and Traveling.

To my two beautiful daughters - Robin and Katie who are between the ages of 25 and 27 years old,

Know that: you have taught me more about life than I could ever teach you. When you were born, I learned what unconditional love was all about. The most important thing in my life is to be a good father. So I share these words with you from the bottom of my heart.

The top values that I encourage for you are:

GET A STRONG EDUCATION
Pursue a strong education – don't stop at your Bachelors – strive for a Masters, perhaps even a PhD, or some certifications. A good education will open doors that may otherwise never open – will provide more opportunities - will give you more confidence – will help in making good choices - will help you get the most out of life.

KEEP A GOOD WORK ETHIC
Work hard – work smart - but work – give back – be a team player - Make your financial decisions using your brain – make your emotional decisions using your heart and never the opposite. Keep good records –

STOP AND SMELL THE ROSES
Experience life – as much as possible – make your world large – explore – laugh, cry, savor every emotion - don't forfeit free time – savor it – spend it wisely – you will never get it back. Plan for the future but live in the present.

BE WITH GOOD PEOPLE
Choose your company carefully. Surround your life with good people. You are influenced by the company you keep – yes, you truly are – we all are. Life is too short to fall victim of other's misdirection. Stay focused on the good things in life – and strive to do good yourself. Life is about making decisions – day in and day out – some big – some small – some have significant impact on our lives –

some do not – never let negative people sway your decisions.

DO THE NEXT RIGHT THING

Be well rounded – do many different things - have many spokes on your wheel of life and may it spin smoothly and freely as a gyroscope in perfect balance. May that balance provide you strength and support for a smooth ride in life. Sow good seeds – many good seeds. You do that by doing the right thing one step at a time.

Make good decisions - Just do the next right thing. Then the next. Then the next.

All my love,
Dad

Paul Ketterer
Born 1954
Newport Catholic High School
University of Kentucky
Ohio of College of Applied Science
Northern KY University
(Business Management)
Corporate Manager (35 yrs)
Magician –
        International Brotherhood
        of Magicians
        Fellowship of
        Christian Magicians
Motivational Speaker
Ballroom Dancing
TV Producer, Author

To my three children Kim, Jayme, and Chip,

Know that: I have raised you all to become <u>individuals</u> and not COPY CATS. We have few leaders in our country and I am very proud you have become individual thinkers and not always followers. I have succeeded to encourage you to "March to a Different Drummer - to be your own person". Everything I have taught you is pretty easy to understand. You lived by most of these saying. I have tried to **KISS** (<u>K</u>eep <u>I</u>t <u>S</u>imple <u>S</u>tupid). Trying to teach you the lesson I have learned.   Hopefully you will remember and think of these sayings before you leap.

The top values that I encourage for you are:

PRAY EVERY NIGHT
Ask God to help you make a success of your life. Ask God to solve your problems and thank Him. Our God wishes to help you, all you have to do is ask.

DO UNTO OTHERS AS YOU WOULD HAVE THEM DO TO YOU
This really needs no explanation; however if someone hurts you don't try to hurt them. They will hurt themselves in the future.

DO IT NOW – DO IT RIGHT – DO IT RIGHT NOW
This is pretty self-explanatory too. Do not put off things, get them finished and do them to the best of your ability. In other words do not procrastinate.

PIGS GET FAT – HOGS GO TO SLAUGHTER
Simply stated: always try to do your best but do not do anything that is unfair to others. Don't take the last piece of pie. In business if you are profitable do not be greedy and try and raise your prices more. Be fair to yourself and fair to your customers.

YOU GET OUT OF PEOPLE WHAT YOU INSPECT NOT WHAT YOU EXPECT
If you are to become a leader remember always to check up on the orders you give to others. In business this is called follow up. Always follow up on things you have asked to be done. Set the example and importance of follow up for other people in your organization.

ONLY FOOLS AND IDIOTS NEVER CHANGE THEIR MIND
Remember your thinking may have flaws too. Listen to others - they might have a better idea. Then change your mind; don't be hardheaded.

A TREE DIES FROM THE TOP DOWN
As a leader you must set the example and others will follow. If the leader has bad habits the organization will pick them up.

YOU CAN CATCH MORE FLIES WITH HONEY THAN YOU CAN WITH VINEGAR
Be nice to people. Compliment when a job is well done and if the job is done poorly relate to them how they might do it differently but be tactful.

IF YOU FOLLOW A CART OF GOLD, YOU WILL PICK UP GOLD. IF YOU FOLLOW A CART OF DIRT YOU WILL PICK UP DIRT
Choose you friends wisely –

YOU SELDOM GET A SECOND CHANCE TO MAKE A FIRST IMPRESSION
Be clean, neat and look good in your appearance every day. Smile and be polite.

TRY EVEYTHING ONCE
If you don't like it try it again. i.e.. eating asparagus, broccoli, etc.

All my love, Dad

P.S. Remember your father and mother as they grow old
   -   they will always love you.

Ken Klosterman
Klosterman Bakery - CEO – Owner
Magician –
   Past International President of
   International Brotherhood of Magicians
   Society of American Magicians
   Collector
Proprietor of Salon De Magie
(World Class Magic Museum)

To Matthew, Adam, and Amy who are between the ages of 17 and 23 years old,

Know that: parenting doesn't come with a manual, and your mother and I have done our very best to raise you with all the love and affection that we could. We have given you everything that we feel you need, and we ask that you work diligently towards the things that you want, and hopefully we have never left you wanting. We love you very much and we can't wait to see you raise families of your own.

The top values that I encourage for you are:

DECISIONS AND GOALS
Live your life by rules. Set rules and boundaries for yourselves and set goals for yourselves. Make decisions that fit what you want to do, who you want to be, and who you want people to see you as being. Your life may take many avenues and what you cannot control is what happens after decisions are made. If you make bad decisions that lead to bad results, then those scars will be there forever. You can do your very best to overcome them, and only time will do that, but you need to be very thoughtful about the decisions that you make.

KINDNESS
My own parents always used to say, "Be careful and be kind to the people that you meet on the way up because you will meet those same people on the way down." I am, hopefully, still on my way up! And I look forward to meeting new people all the time.

DO YOUR BEST
My goal is to make it through day-by-day doing the very best that I can. Try to do things right the first time, and, again, it is not possible all the time, but if you strive to do things right the first time, you will make fewer mistakes. Also, you will have fewer regrets that you need to apologize for. Don't be afraid to apologize if you make a

mistake: it is human; no one is perfect. It is those people who are never wrong who continue to make enemies and make life hard for themselves. If you pretend to be perfect, then you obviously aren't.

DREAMS

Time is important in relation to goals. We talk all the time about setting goals and aspiring to reach those heights, but I think that you have to dream your whole life. If you stop dreaming you stop reaching for the stars.

Love,
Dad

Bruce Kozerski
Born: 1962
Education:
College of the Holy Cross, MA
(Physics)
Wooster College Tech, MA
(Mechanical
      Engineering)
Married to Elizabeth for 27
years
Career:
Bengal's Football (12 seasons)
      Drafted in 1984:
Pro football broadcaster on
Cincinnati Bengals network
Contractor in construction
High School sports coach
High School math teacher
Hobbies: fishing and hunting

To my two delightful daughters of age 16 and 20,

Know that: I love you and I am so very proud of you. I want you to grow up to be healthy, wise, and financially strong enough to live a comfortable life. I want you to find happiness, contentment, and a peaceful harmony in your lives.

The top values that I encourage for you are:

LUCK
I want you to be lucky enough to be the one chosen: the one left standing when others have failed; the one who gets the best education; the one who gets all the comforts of life.

I want you to be lucky enough to get a good spouse: one that truly loves you, respects you, is kind to you, one that helps you to be a better person.

I want you to be lucky enough to be at the right place at the right time and certainly not the wrong place at the wrong time.

I want you to be lucky like Jessie Owens, one of the finest athletes, who was discovered and trained: not like his brother who actually was a faster runner, but who fell into the wrong crowd, and took a much less desirable path in life.

I want you to be lucky enough to learn and to live each day with life's most basic lessons: eat right, get at least 7 hours sleep, exercise at least 30 minutes, reduce stress, and keep good blood flow.

I want you to be lucky enough to earn respect and to respect those that have earned it: to receive kindness and to spread kindness.

I want you to be lucky enough to learn something new everyday.

I want you to be lucky enough to be happy every day and to spread happiness every day.

All my love,
Dad

P.S. Luck is what fools call it when God gives them a break. So don't do stupid things. Keep your nose straight. Love and obey God with all your heart and he will provide you with all the luck you will ever need.

Anonymous
Born 1967

A THOUGHT FROM THE DAD'S CORNER
"We must believe in luck. For how else can we explain the success of those we don't like?"
Jean Cocteau (1889 – 1963)

To Marisa (of age 7), Connor (of age 5), and Tyler (of age 3),

Know that: my life would have never been complete without you. Each of you showed me new ways to laugh, love, cry and think.   You constantly challenge me to be a better father, husband and person. Hearing your voice energizes me, watching you learn is captivating and feeding your curiosities is a relentless task that I cherish every day. I consider myself the luckiest man on earth to be married to the woman I love and to be raising the three of you.

The top values that I encourage for you are:

ALWAYS DO YOUR BEST
My high school basketball coach once told me that practice doesn't make perfect, "Perfect practice makes perfect". As I go through life I constantly remind myself of this. Try to produce your best always in no matter what your endeavor and no matter what the situation. You will never lose if you give every ounce of effort you have and you can never be ashamed if you don't succeed so long as you know you could have absolutely done nothing more. Here is the catch, only you will know if you gave your full effort.

RECOVERY
Everyone makes mistakes; everyone has setbacks in life, careers and schooling. Your life will be defined by how well you overcome these setbacks, not on the setbacks themselves. You will learn more about yourself, your friends and your family at these times than when you are successful.

BALANCE YOUR LIFE
There are so many things that will entertain you as you grow. Explore your curiosities, while continuing to work and study hard. Make time for friends and family while

ensuring that you have quiet time to read and travel. Try not to let one part of your life monopolize all your time.

BE DECISIVE
You will make better decisions the more information you have. Do not be afraid to ask questions, to respectfully question others, to research and to weigh the pros and cons. Know that in the end, each decision is yours and you must make them timely and decisively. The freedom of choice is a right that should be cherished and protected; don't let others take this away from you.

SURROUND YOURSELF WITH GOOD PEOPLE
The reason most people are successful is because they have an innate ability to keep good company. A good person is one who will tell you they disagree with you and not be afraid to listen to you when you disagree with them. Always be honest, fair, objective and consistent and look for the same in others. Keep good company and your chance of success in life, love and business will increase tenfold and you will be happier as a bonus.

Love,
Dad

 Darren Leary
Born: 1974
Turpin High School (Cincinnati, OH)
University of Evansville – BA
Keller Graduate School of Management (MBA)
General Contractor Commercial Construction
Hobbies: Golfing, Triathlons, Home Improvements, Hiking, Skiing, Reading, Traveling

To my two remarkable sons Darren and Colin and my delightful grandchildren Marisa, Connor and Tyler, and Susan a very special daughter-in-law,

Know that: your mom and I treasure each moment we have had, do have and will have with you. Family is what we live for and you have made us happy beyond all the words I can find to express our love. I am not sure when I realized it but this opportunity to give you advice has clarified something I have known for a long time. That is that you both have grown in remarkable ways and really no longer need my advice. I watch you and I am proud. Sometime in the future I will be in need of your advice and I hope I will know to accept it from the wise men that you are.

The top values that I encourage for you are:

FAMILY
Our family is the foundation of all we do. It is why we do things. It is the core of all the things we trust and believe in. Cherish each moment you have with your family and work hard to grow it. Often times it is not easy. Your patience will wear thin. Decisions will be difficult. Emotions will be frayed. Finances will be difficult. The outcome will strengthen the fabric of your family and provide you great satisfaction in the future.

RESPONSIBILITY
You have great gifts in intellect, personality and leadership. You have worked hard to develop them. It is a responsibility to use them well. Invest them in the people who work for you, use their labor wisely and your contribution will be multiplied. Invest them in your peers because you expect the same from them. Invest your talents in your superiors and they will develop other opportunities for you. Invest your gifts in your community to make this a better place to live.

INTEGRITY
What you do is who you are. Thoughts can develop, change and mature. What you say and what you do are permanent. Words and actions have a long lasting effect, good as well as bad, on the people around you. Be wise and thoughtful about how you affect other people.

HISTORY
You knew this would be part of it! Read autobiographies and historical novels. Make it a habit to read historical markers whenever you can. It will give the kids something to talk about, that is for sure. Look around at the terrain. Appreciate the difficulties that were encountered that caused the marker to be important. Try to understand the decisions that had to be made to achieve success. Think about the resources that were available at that time. Consider how important that effort was at that time and what it would mean today if that had not happened. It will give you a measure, an order of magnitude, of the role we each can play to make the world better.

FINALLY
Play catch with your kids for as long as you can. You will remember and treasure that for a lifetime.

Love,
Dad

Patrick R. Leary   Born 1946
Married to Melinda (41 yrs)
Francis Jordan High School
    Milwaukee WI
Embry Riddle University:
    BS Aviation Management
Drexel University - MBA Finance
US Army 1966-72 - Helicopter Pilot
Hobbies and interest:
Grandchildren, Bicycling, Flying,
History, Veterans Volunteer
Services.

To My beautiful Newborn Baby Girl, Ella (11 weeks),

Know that: I had tears of joy in my eyes when you were born. I was so happy to finally see you, meet you, hold you, and kiss you after nine long months. Know that shortly after you were born I telephoned your great grandmother, along with your grandma and grandpa and described you simply as being "perfect." My love for you and your mother is immense. Know that I am blessed to have you both in my life and I will always be there for you in this world and the next. I love you.

The top values that I encourage for you are:
FAMILY
Just 11 weeks old and you are well aware of who your mommy and daddy are, especially your mommy when it is time to eat! Never forget how loved you are by your family. Both sets of your grandparents attempt to be the first to hold you during visits. You have three loving aunts that already have begun to spoil you and a mother who thinks the world of you. And then there is me. I had promised myself I would not be one of those fathers who show countless photographs of their children to co-workers and friends. Well, I am here to tell you I have broken that promise. In fact, I can't wait to show you off to all. Life will be busy for you in the distant future. Don't forget to make time to reach out to your loved ones. Family will be there for you during your times of need just like you will be there for theirs.
EDUCATION
Education is of the utmost importance. Your father learned this much later in life than he should have. If I could go back in time I would take my high school Geometry class, my pre-requisite college Biology course and academics in general more seriously. Ella, education aids you in becoming a well- rounded individual. It teaches discipline, how to interact with others, time management and so much more. Always remember that education is the one thing that can never be taken away from you!

WORK ETHIC
Your great-grandfather and great-grandmother passed on the commitment to work ethic to your grandpa. Your grandpa and grandma then passed on the importance of having a hard work ethic to me. I too will strive to teach you never to give up on your goals and always give 110% in everything you do. Your dedication to work will represent you and what you stand for. With that said, choose a career that you will enjoy, one that you will look forward to tackling daily. A large part of your life will be dedicated to your chosen career. Make the most of it, Ella. Do not worry so much as to what your salary will be at any said job. With work ethic and dedication, your success, both from a fulfillment standpoint and a monetary standpoint will follow.

FAITH AND PROVIDING ASSISTANCE TO THOSE LESS FORTUNATE
Ella, I have never been the most religious person to walk the earth but I do believe in God. Ella, have faith in God throughout your life. Donate your time and energy to the less fortunate when able to do so. There will be numerous people you encounter throughout your life that will genuinely need a helping hand. Doing so will energize your spirit and faith in mankind.

CLOSING THOUGHTS
Some other important values include: Have pride in our country and the sacrifices others have made for our freedom. Always be honest as one lie creates many more. Be a good neighbor. Pay attention to detail, as there are plenty that don't. Demonstrate respect for elders. Dress to impress (shoes shined, pants creased and having a straight gig line) and remember it is always better to attend an event overdressed than underdressed when unsure of what to wear. There is so much more but you will pick it up along the way. I know that down the road your mother and I will be so proud of you. Eleven weeks in, we already are.

I love you Ella. –Dad
(Scott Lengle - See Scott's photo and bio on page 136)

To my courageous daughter of age 25,

Know that: I love you with my whole being and I am so very, very proud of you. You have become such a strong, independent and beautiful adult, and now soon to be a parent yourself. Your mother and I hope and pray that our new grandchild will be born healthy – with all ten fingers and toes. We are here for you as parents and soon as grandparents to help you in any way that you need. We are so happy, relieved and proud of you for having the discipline to wait for the appropriate time to have your child. You are now in the position to be a good parent and I know that you will be.

The top values that I encourage for you are:
There are so many topics to share with you but these two below seem to be the timeliest right now.

BE PATIENT WITH YOUR CHILDREN
Be patient with your children – it takes a long time for them to grow up. It's not an easy process – for them or for you. They will be so very challenging at times. They will test your patience – test your patience – and test your patience again. I know you know this but it can never be said too many times: NEVER SHAKE YOUR BABY. One of the most challenging times I ever had with you was what I referred to as your curing time. Through your early 20's you floundered in your direction in life. Nothing I could say would help. You didn't want to listen to me – you didn't want any of my guidance. The only thing I could do was to be patient with you and quietly observe while you found your path making many mistakes that I could have helped you avoid. That was extremely painful and tough on me. But I am thankful that somewhere, somehow I mustered up enough patience to silently wait in the wings for you to cure. And you did – and I am so very proud of you for finding your way. Yes – many, many challenges – but it was worth every one of them.

DON'T SPOIL YOUR CHILDREN

Don't spoil your children – let your mother and I, as grandparents, do that. That's what we, as grandparents, plan to do, and plan to do very well. That's just part of being grandparents. But don't you, as parents, spoil your children. Spoiled children are a pain to be around and even worse when they become supposedly adults. They often become very controlling, disrespectful and sometimes even deceitful. It's not the children's fault – the parents are the ones to blame – it's the parents who spoiled them. We have tried to raise you by the motto "Give a person a fish and you feed him for a day – Teach a person how to fish and you feed him for a life time". And it has worked very well for us. You cannot give discipline but discipline needs to be taught, learned and lived. Discipline is a lifetime survival tool. Teach them to say "Please" and "Thank You" and say it sincerely – just as you have learned. Your mother and I were never quite sure how much is too much to give to you. One barometer we used was to observe your attitudes and when you stopped appreciating and saying "thank you" we stopped giving. It seems now a days that many young parents sacrifice discipline under the guise of avoiding thwarting off creativity in their children. I say a little more discipline and a little less creativity is not all bad. Your children can have both if you parent them right.

Love,
Dad

Anonymous
Born 1958

To Rose Ann, Raymond, Randy, Rosalie and Richard, our full house (3 kings and 2 queens) of ages between 52 and 42.

Know that: your mother (now deceased) and I have been successful in life and live/lived the Christian values that you were taught. I never tried to drum my values into your heads, but chose a path that would teach you good Christian values by example.

SPEND TIME WITH YOUR FAMILY – BUILD MEMORIES –

Along your paths in life, I guided you everyday by involving you in activities, some serious and some playful, which were important to your mother and I.

One of our passions was Magic. We were serious about being the best we could be. Our life together started with an engagement ring tied to a silk scarf produced at the end of my presentation at one of the annual magic picnics, followed by our honeymoon at the combined IBM-SAM Convention in Chicago.

As you magically appeared, we involved you in the show, performed as "Mr. E. and Rene", and rewarded you with our annual trip to the Abbott Magic Get-together each year. A couple of you still claim that you could do the lines for the whole show. Richard earned extra money by making balloon animals after our shows. Rose Ann filled in as my assistant when mom was unavailable. Randy, Raymond and Rosalie toted equipment when necessary.

The major breadwinner for the family was my career in the United States Postal Service. I worked for Uncle Sam for 37 years, most of them as a letter carrier. I was on the same route for 22 years, before entering supervision. It was not unusual on Saturdays or during the summer to see several of you tagging along as I delivered my mail route. After sorting my mail, we headed for the local donut shop, and later it was at my mom's, or the pizza place for lunch.

A really fun adventure that you kids still talk about, even today, was the Sunday morning Amtrak train chases. After church, we headed to River Road and followed Amtrak to Indiana, where we always ended up with a carload of fresh baked goods. A popular spot at home was the basement where we built a 20' x 30' HO model railroad layout, which you were able to run at an early age. After retiring from the Postal Service, I went to work for the Indiana & Ohio railroad as an engineer, and this gave all you kids the opportunity to ride on the big ones, particularly the excursion trips out of Lebanon, Ohio. Many of our vacations were built around doing magic shows and visiting short line railroads across the United States and Canada, and the five of you young-ins were always ready to pile in the car for some adventure.

Much of my spare time was involved in the printing business that I owned and operated. This operation also provided many opportunities for the family to participate as a group. Your mother did all the typesetting and everyone else got involved with folding, collating and stapling. Ray learned to run the presses, and helped run the church bulletins while we were performing shows.

Love, Dad

Ron Maifeld
Born 1939
Elder High School
2nd Language – Spanish
U.S. Post Office
Indiana and Ohio Railroad
Owner – Operator of Ralph Printing Co.
Magician – AKA
         "Mr. E & Rene"
        "Professor of
          Pandemonious Prestidigitation"

To my three children Holli, Zachary, and Molly, who are between the ages of 7 and 21,

Know that: I love you, my three kids, and you all have done such a great job. Holli, you went to a Christian school and are now a junior at Texas Technical University. You are majoring in nutrition, on the honor roll, and are doing great – you are a great young lady. Zach, now in the 4th grade, and Molly, in the 2nd grade, at Calvary Christian School - are passionate about your schoolwork and all the programs there. You both are also doing so well in school. Also, you both are very passionate and love to win at soccer, and like your dad, you are just competitive in all sports. I'm glad that we all go to church and are very dedicated to Calvary Baptist Church in Latonia.

The top values that I encourage for you are:

EDUCATION
Education is very important. Holli, you are doing very well at Texas Tech with your grades, and I feel that Zach and Molly, you should do the same kind of things. Go and get as much education as possible. It is statistically proven in life that kids who go to school and get a further education do better in life income-wise, and they do not struggle as much. Education is something that is very important.

HUMILITY
Be kind to others and be humble. There are so many people out there without a lot of humility, especially in sports, and people are choosing the wrong things. Zach, you and I love to watch sports. I think being kind and being humble and doing good things out there with your talents is very important.

CHRISTIANITY
Stay close to God. My dad is a pastor, and has been a pastor all his life. And when I was growing up, he would always say that "Men will fail you, but God will never fail

you." I am a Christian. And Jesus came into my heart at a young age. And I am glad that you children, Holli, Zach, and Molly, are also Christians. When the times get tough and things don't always go right in your life, you can always lean on God and His word - the Bible. And He will always bring you through.

FINANCIAL

Live within your means. As an investment advisor, I work with people everyday on their finances and how to grow their money, save their money and spend their money wisely. I counsel people when they get into trouble on how to get out of trouble. Try not to always want so much. And save your money and be able to pay cash for things. Take care of the financial things without living on credit. One of the biggest faults today in our society is people living on credit. And the main thing is that they cannot control their passions and their wants, and they think they have got to have it now. That is a huge part of a lot of people's issues in life and failures--- not being able to control their impulses and impulse buying and shopping. Always look at saving money and, of course, as Christians, our first 10% of our income as Christians is to give money back to the church, give back to God, and if you live by that principle, then you will always be taken care of.

Love, Dad

Danny McNeill
Born: 1964
Education:
Pelasky Cnty High School, Dublin, VA
Liberty University, Lynchburg, VA
Married to Paula for 14 years
Career: Banker - Alexandria Financial
Center Manager
Hobbies: golf, soccer, coaching for my
children, all sports

To my three sons, Curry Jr. age 54, Gregory age 52, and Mark age 50,

Know that: I am proud of your successes; you are all good men. Though your mother and I were divorced when Curry Jr. was about 16, you all have earned your way through life very well and I am proud of you for it. Again, you are all good men, and I love you, and I know that you are giving it your best so that you are the best that you can be.

The top values that I encourage for you are:

EDUCATIONAL ADVANCES
You all have had some college, and I am glad that you have attained more of an education than I have—this is what I wanted for you. You are all on your own now and have earned your way through things and are good men.

BE HONEST AND TRUTHFUL
I have always encouraged you to be honest and truthful and I have been that way with you, and you have been that way with me. When you turned eighteen, I wrote a letter individually to you and told you that now you are on your own, but I would always be there for you, to help you in any way that I could. You have been very faithful that way and very appreciative.

FINANCIAL CHOICES
I have always encouraged you to be able to pay for what you want and need and not go into debt too much. In your businesses you have been fortunate and have done well and have fended for yourselves very well.

RELIGION
You have all been brought up in church and with closeness to church. Religion is always something that we have done as a family, and it is good that you stay active in church.

Love, Dad

Curry Meece
Born 1937
Education: Hughes High School
Mechanical engineer/ Assembler / Machinist
Hobbies: Singing and Kite flying

A THOUGHT FROM THE DAD'S CORNER
"Fortune does not change men, it unmasks them."
Suzanne Necker (1739 – 1794)

To my four children, Angela, Michael, Laura Beth, and Tim, who are between the ages of 25 and 35 years old,

Know that: raising children is the most challenging job you may ever have, yet the rewards are outstanding. All of you are a gift from God but not one of you came with instructions and that's where the challenge came in. So I learned as you grew. As a Dad I've made mistakes. And as I look back I regret them, but I only did what I thought was best for you at the time. I tried to teach you life lessons only to realize now that what I wanted to teach you was something that you must experience yourself and learn on your own. There have been times in my life when each one of you has said or done something that has made me realize that some of the things I tried to teach have stayed with you. It may have been a conversation or a 3 a.m. phone call just to tell me how much you love me. These things mean a lot to me. Always know that each of you are special and that I'm proud of you and I will always love you now and forever.

The top values that I encourage for you are:

NEVER FORGET

1. Who you are.

2. Where you came from.

3. To think about what you do before you do it.

4. To accept Responsibility for your own actions.

5. This is Mom and Dad's house but it is always your home.

6. To never borrow trouble.

7. To put your faith in God for He will take care of you.

8. To not underestimate the power of prayer.

9. You can never say I love you too often.

With all my love,

Dad

Randy Norris
Born 1953
Married to Peggy for 36 years
Career: Machinist
Hobbies and interest:
Magician,
Baking with my Grandchildren

A THOUGHT FROM THE DAD'S CORNER
"Pray as if everything depended upon God and work as if everything depended upon man."
Francis Cardinal Spellman (1889 – 1967)

To my wonderful son of age 29,

Know that: I am so very proud of you and that I love you. You have grown into a fine and responsible young man and I truly appreciate that you seem to listen to me more now. You don't have to take my advice but just allowing me to share it with you makes me feel like I'm part of your life.

The top values that I encourage for you are:

DON'T FIND OUT THE HARD WAY
Remember – Never pour grease down your kitchen sink. ☺ Learning from your mistakes is good but learning from someone else's mistakes is even better.

NORMAL
What's normal -Who gets to decide? – Our society and the people around you, that your trust, have a very strong influence on what you think is normal. So the people around you often set the norms in your life. Make sure they are good people.

WAITING
The art of waiting is to keep busy. While you are waiting for your ship to come in - send out more ships. If you don't send out any ships few will come back in. "Don't put all your eggs in one basket" applies more to than just finances.
While you are waiting is an ideal time to make self improvements: whether big like going back to college or small like doing exercises while you are waiting for the game to come on. In a nutshell, don't waste time waiting – keep busy in the process. Make the best of the time in front of you.

CHANGE
Change is inevitable. The rate of change keeps increasing. Change is often difficult so you will find it a lot easier to change yourself when appropriate than to try and change those around you. Look at your own shortcomings and work on those first.

TRUST

Be careful when you take advice from someone that has an agenda – from someone who is trying to sell you something, from someone that has something to gain. I have found, in general, there are usually three sides to the story – His truth, her truth, and the truth somewhere in the middle. I tend to favor the one in the middle. Beware of half-truths. Half-truths often are 80 to 90% true with a bit of fallacies sprinkled in. Half-truths are the toughest and sneakiest ones to see through. They're the most persuasive.

Love,
Dad

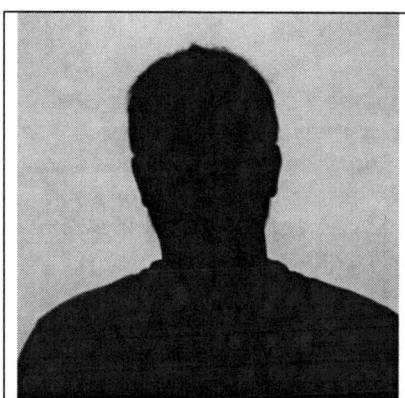

Anonymous
Born 1959

A THOUGHT FROM THE DAD'S CORNER
"Do not trust all men, but trust men of worth; the former course is silly, the latter a mark of prudence." **Democritus (460 BC - 370 BC)**

To my *first* daughters Ruth and Rachel and then my *second* daughters Brittany and Megan who are between the ages 18 to 35,

Know that: even before God created the world, He knew and loved all of you. I am so thankful you are in His hands.

The top values I encourage for you are:

SEARCH YOURSELF EVERY DAY
The values that God put inside you are the only absolutes in life. They will never change and they will never steer you wrong. Always be honest with yourself and pursue what you instinctively know is right. Never make excuses for not following this *natural law* God endowed you with.

ACT FOR OTHERS
Those who live their lives helping others and who are legitimately concerned about their welfare are the happiest people on earth. Every second you spend trying to make someone else's life better lights up your soul. There is no greater goal you can set for yourself. Although you may not be looking for rewards, God will shower you with them.

REFUSE TO SEE EVIL
This is so hard, because there is so much evil in the world, but you cannot allow yourself to become infected by it. Always think *good* first and never look for revenge. Remember, no matter how bad some things may seem, the balance is always tipped in the other direction. Knights in white armor and conquering heroes do exist and evil will be defeated.

THERE ARE ANGELS
You are never alone. God gave you angels to protect you. I truly believe this. If you open your heart you can feel them around you every second of the day. Sometimes you can even see them and talk to them, but you won't

even know they were angels until later. There is no such thing as luck or coincidence. There is a reason for everything.

GOD DOES LOVE YOU

You sang songs like "*Jesus Loves me this I know*" when you were little girls. Never grow up.
Never think that kind of childhood innocence is silly. It is the only reality that matters. Your Faith is your life, strength and happiness. The way I love you with every ounce of my being as your earthly father is the way your heavenly Father cherishes you.

MIRACLES DO HAPPEN!

You all know you have a *magic* dad. I hope more than anything that I have taught you miracles are not just for the stage. The world may seem to be hard and cruel at times, but there is another world right there in plain sight that is a magic place full of wonder and splendor. It is a world where your deepest hopes and dreams will come true. Have unrelenting belief in miracles and they will become your reality.

Love, Daddy

Richard Osterlind
Born: 1948
Married to Lisa for 12 years
Education:
Western Connecticut State University
   (Major – Music: Percussion)
Career: International Mentalist
   (based in Northern Kentucky)
Hobbies: Music, shooting sports, reading

To my son Matt of age 25,

Know that: Being a father has been my best job, my toughest job and my most important job. I have no idea how I did. I'll leave that up to you. I work in a world of prepared scripts, teleprompters and careful editing. But being a dad is a lifetime of ad-libs.

My humble suggestions as you go through life:

BE HONEST
It allows you to sleep at night. You've always been honest to a fault. Don't change. Sometimes it's painful. Especially with the IRS.

DO WHAT "YOU" THINK IS RIGHT
Let your conscience be your guide. Don't be swayed by friends, politics or popular opinion. If it's against the grain, so what? You'll be able to live with yourself.

BE RESPECTFUL
It never goes out of style. A simple kind or encouraging word makes others feel better, and it's amazing how good it will also make you feel.

BE HELPFUL
We're not here very long; so don't be selfish with your time, talents or efforts.

KEEP YOUR SENSE OF HUMOR
You have a talent for making people laugh. George Carlin and Richard Pryor are dead and the world is sorely in the need of a few more yucks.

DON'T TAKE YOURSELF TOO SERIOUSLY
Have some fun. Pete Gillen used to say "No man on his death bed ever uttered 'I wish I would have spent more time at the office.'" Agreed.

DO YOUR BEST
I don't care what you choose to do, just give it your best shot. There's a lot of satisfaction in doing a job well.

KEEP THE FAITH AND LOVE YOUR FAMILY
It's why we do the things we do.

Love, Dad

John Popovich
Born: 1950
Struthers High School
Ohio University
Bachelors in Telecommunications
Married for 38 years to Kathie
Sports Director at WCPO TV
Hobbies and interest: Reading, Cooking, working around the house

A THOUGHT FROM THE DAD'S CORNER
"A sense of humor is part of the art of leadership, of getting along with people, of getting things done." **Dwight D. Eisenhower (1890 – 1969)**

To my wonderful children Melissa (of age 36), Matthew (of age 34) and Jeff (of age 29)

Know that: you, along with your mother, are the joys of my life and are cherished beyond words. I am incredibly proud of the adults you have become.

The top values that I encourage for you are:

FINANCIAL SECURITY
This is a long term commitment but one that is necessary. You have a family that depends on you and they need to be protected. Make sure you have adequate insurance coverage, emergency money available, and a long-term financial plan in place that includes a will. Life is not fair so you need to be prepared for all the surprises you'll encounter. Have a Plan B so you can weather the storms life throws at you. Luck favors the prepared. Know the difference between a want and a need. You don't need to live a Spartan life but do prioritize where to spend your money. Do make sure to take vacations. Make them special so you'll have lasting memories that make you smile whenever they are recalled.

HAPPINESS
Be happy with your life, with your spouse and your children. Laugh every day. Smile and sing often. Do the right thing. Be honest, be fair, be kind, be polite, be forgiving, be tolerant, and be courteous. Life is a gift and everyday is special. Make the most of it. Count your blessings.

KNOWLEDGE/EDUCATION
Never stop learning. Read a newspaper, a book, follow current events. Be informed about the world you live in and your children's world. Know their friends and what they are doing. Learn new skills and develop new hobbies. You will be amazed at what you can achieve and have fun

while you're at it. You'll be a more interesting person and that is a good thing.

WORK ETHIC
Work hard. Hard work tends to be rewarded. Take pride in everything you do. Be a dependable and productive worker as others are counting on you. Take satisfaction from a job well done. Be respectful and nice to the people you work with. My hope is that you love your work. But always remember why it's called work.

FAMILY
Your family provides unconditional love and support. Home and family is your oasis and safe haven. You will always be safe and secure among your family. Provide this sense of love, safety and security for yourself, your mate and your children. Life is tough enough and one must have a safe place to hide sometimes.

Love always,
Dad

Bob Quallick
Born 1948
Married to Eileen 1971
B.S. Mechanical Engineering
      Lehigh University - 1970
MBA – Hofstra University - 1977
Sales & Sales Management -
      Industrial Machinery
Industry
Hobbies: Gardening, Travel, Golf, Cooking, Reading

To my son Kirk, of age 24,

Know that: the deep love that I have for you, you may not even know until you yourself become a parent. Once you are a parent and have a son, you will realize this deep love, too. Even though you are 24, I still care about you, worry about you, as much as I did when you were first born. I still always want to help you out and nurture you along, and I want only the best for you.

The top values that I encourage for you are:

BE A GOOD PERSON
Instilled in me by my father is the idea of being a good person. Be true to yourself and respectful of others, as you would want them to be respectful of you. It comes down to the old saying of: Treat everybody as you would like for them to treat you.

BE HONEST AND UPRIGHT
You can have all the money in the world and material possessions to go with it, but once you lose your reputation or character or the type of person you are, then you don't get that back   Life to me is all about who you are, the type of person you can be. And, obviously, it starts with the type of character that you have and the type of life you live.

BE REALISTIC
Sometimes the biggest challenge as a parent is being overprotective, building up too many walls, keeping you shaded from the realities of life. You hear people say all the time that you can be whatever you want to be. The stark reality is that - that is not always the case. You should always do the best that you can do. Then let the chips fall where they may. You may not always get the job even though you are the most qualified. The good guys do not always win. The guys in the white hats do not always ride out into the sunset being the victors. I am not a negative person, but you have to set yourself up to be able to deal with the adversities of life. Anyone can handle success, but the true measure, or character of a

person, is how you deal with adversity. To me, that separates the men from the boys.

KNOW YOUR GIFTS

Each individual has their own sets of skills and they have certain special traits. You should know your own special traits that are unique to you, and build on your own individual and God-given talents. Sometimes these talents are hidden within yourself. That is the key—to unlock and use your own talents.

SET CAREER AND LIFE GOALS

Learn as much as you can about whatever it is that you are doing. Again, give it your best. Know that the learning experience is a lifetime commitment. It is something that is ongoing. Knowing relationship and networking ethics is very important to anyone today. Also, don't limit yourself to only one vocation. That is, always have an A, B, and C plan so that you have more than one option out there. So many people look only at short-term goals instead of looking at the big picture down the line, at long-term goals. Have your sets of goals to work towards and it will keep you focused. See what is beyond the horizon and not just what is here today. We live in a push-button technology world and everything is instantaneous. Yet the reality of it is that we have to look beyond today and look toward tomorrow.

Love,
Dad

Mark Shufflebarger
Born 1955
Northern Kentucky University
Cincinnati Financial Corp 25 yrs
HOBBIES – Reading, Sports, Music
Collect antique radios and art deco,
Gym member.

To my sons Brady of age 9 and Lucas of age 5,

Know that: long ago, I met a beautiful girl, and within a few months, I knew she was the one. So I asked her to marry me. I always wanted to have a family and be a father. At age 28 I was now ready to be one.

When Brady was born he wasn't breathing. They called in all different medical people and I was scared to death. I had no idea what was going on and had to try to keep a strong face for my your mother's sake. I was praying like crazy, and after about four minutes, they finally cleared his breathing canal. That was the longest four minutes of my life.
The same thing happened to Lucas when he was born. Since your mother was having a 'C' section this time, we were warned he wouldn't be breathing right away.

You both have taught me so much and keep me young and active. I love to share my time with you, playing in the yard or even jumping on the trampoline when it's not too cold outside. I just tucked you both in and we said a prayer to "give us tomorrow."

I remember having lots of fun with my own father (and we still do). My father has taught me how to love and raise two very precious boys of my own. All four of us are very close.

What I want you to remember is how much time we got to spend together: All those vacations we went on; all the camping trips with the four wheelers; and all the fun times we spent with our family and friends. Remember when you wanted me to be a professional wrestler until you found out I would have to travel and would hardly get to see you.

I hope I am doing a good job raising you and teaching you what's right and wrong in life. I hope you will take these memories, and some day, pass them on to your family. I hope you will have as much fun as I did. I hope you will always want to go jump on the trampoline with me. I love you two and I am so blessed to have you. Thanks for "giving me tomorrow." Everything I do is so you can make your lives the best they can be.

The top values that I encourage for you are:

ENJOY LIFE - Enjoy life every day.
THANK GOD - Thank God every day for what we have and what He has done for you and me.
GO AFTER IT - If you want something - don't wait until tomorrow - go get it today.
BE KIND TO OTHERS - Treat others nicer than you are treated because I believe what goes around comes around. Remember to help others.
MAKE MEMORIES - Take time to make memories and enjoy your life.
DREAM - Dream to make tomorrow a better day.

Love,
Dad

NAME – Jason Smith
Born – 1975
Married to Summer for 9 years
Campbell County High School 1993
Professional Magician
International Brotherhood
of Magicians

To my wonderful son of age 17,

Know that: I love you and I am so very proud of you. There are certain things in life that you cannot and won't understand unless you experience it yourself. For example: You can understand darkness but you cannot understand blindness. You can see the magnificence of fireworks on TV but you cannot know the thrill of them until you experience them in real life. You won't understand fatherhood until you become a father. Being a father is challenging and difficult but it is one of the best things in my life.

The top values that I encourage for you are:

TRUTHS
Always be truthful – sometimes it requires extra tact and skills – but don't lie. I have found a lot less truth in people, even close friends and relatives, than I originally believed was there. And it is often very painful to find out that someone you trust has lied to you. So don't lie.

MOVE OUT OF YOUR COMFORT ZONE
Push your limits – you can do a lot more than you think – just keep pushing a little more each day – just like you do with your exercise. And look how far you have come. Push and strengthen your mind like you push your body.

GROW UP
Grow up – life is hard. Take responsibility for yourself and do what you should do. Put your video games away – or at least play them a lot less. Focus on your life and how you will prepare to handle it as life comes rushing at you – and it will - when you are out on your own – it will.

INFATUATION
Infatuation is usually the first emotion that you encounter in a relationship that starts to develop. It is certainly a beautiful emotion but it is also a double-edged sword: one of beauty – one of blindness. One of the beauties of infatuation is that it's such an emotional high: you can only see the other person's good side; you put your relationship first; you can't wait to be together. It's the

blindness part that scares most parents, including your mother and I. You will learn with time and realize that infatuation does eventually erode leaving you with the reality of whom you really are and what you both really have to offer each other: the test of true love. When infatuation wears thin or is gone, other parts of your lives begin to take priority. You no longer put your relationship first: it begins getting the leftovers. Now, when you are together, you both are exhausted from using your energy on other priorities: now, often less patient and more cranky; now, you have to work at your relationship when before it just seemed to come naturally. I know of no way to capture and hold onto infatuation. It's like carrying a hand full of sand: it slips through your fingers as you move through life. That's why your mother and I look at the girls you bring home differently than the way you do. We know that a healthy, meaningful, and lasting relationship is much more about the substance of the persons involved and a lot less about the outer beauty they may possess.

Love,
Dad

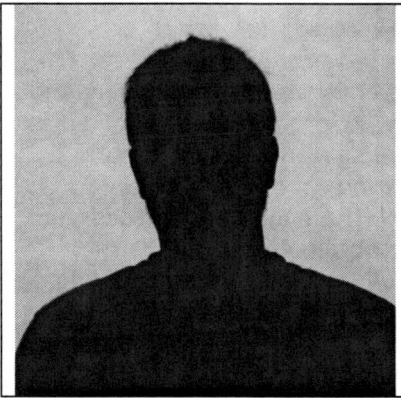

Anonymous
Born 1970

To my children, Jill, Emily, Monica, Theresa, Billy, and Mark,

Know that: For all eternity, it was God's will that I be blessed with the six of you to protect, provide for, raise, and educate as my children. There were times that Mom and I wondered if we would be fortunate enough to have even one child. The opportunity to adopt you four girls, and then, after many years of seeing infertility specialists, to reward our efforts with you two boys, was no doubt a generous response to our humble prayers.

How well did I carry out my calling as a father, God will judge me, but I desired greatly to be a good father, one that encouraged his children to grow into a loving, responsible, selfless, and caring adult.

Of all the things that you may remember about me, I pray that you most remember me as loving you.

The top values that I encourage for you are:

EMBRACE YOUR CATHOLIC FAITH
Your faith in Jesus Christ, your faith in the Catholic Church, is not only to be treasured, but also to be embraced. Life only makes sense, regardless of the difficulties in your path, if it is viewed as an ongoing and continuous journey to know, love, and serve God. Since we are human, and not pure spirits, growing in faith requires our time and effort in prayer and spiritual exercises in order to develop the habits and virtues that each of us must struggle to obtain. Your faith is the greatest gift I wanted to give you, and I pray that you desire it as a great gift for my grandchildren.

STAND UP FOR LIFE
As Pope John Paul II while visiting the United States commanded: "Stand up for life!" Defending the right to life of the most innocent and defenseless member of the human family, the unborn child, is what God is asking all of us to do whether we want to or not. We need to be the

light illuminating the Judeo-Christian principle of the sanctity of all innocent human life, and of the principle that there is no life unworthy to be lived. Many young people are overwhelmed with the fear that a child will cause them a great expense, deny them opportunities and career advancements, require sacrifices of them, and consume their time and energy. By welcoming whatever child or children God may place in your lives, you will give witness to the fact that every child is a gift from God, someone who is precious and unique.

DESIRE TO BE A GOOD PARENT

With whatever child or children God may bless you, desire to be a loving, disciplined, sacrificial, and caring parent. Since children do not come with an owner's manual, there are so many difficult questions for which there are no simple answers that will require your good judgment. Base your decision on what you think is best for your child, and pray that God will grant you and your child the grace you both need on your journey home to Him.

MY FAVORITE QUOTE

As Jesus stated, "To whom much is given much will be expected." To you who have been given life, faith, family, siblings, intelligence, health, opportunities, and love, God will expect much. To the best of your ability, struggle to please Him.

All my love, the man who deeply cares for you - Dad

Fred H. Summe   Born 1949
EDUCATION:
Covington Catholic High School
B.A. - Physics - Thomas More College
J.D. - Chase College of Law
MARRIED to Pam Steltenkamp Summe
CAREER: Attorney at Law, Sole Practitioner for 36 years
SERVICE: Vice President of Northern Kentucky Right to Life
Columnist for *My People*, published by Presentation Ministries, Cincinnati, Oh

To my son Tim and daughter Cindy who are in their 50's,

Know that: I love both of you, no doubt about that. My love for you is hard to describe. You have achieved most of the goals that you have set for yourselves, and I am very satisfied that you have kept yourselves pointed in the right direction. You have tried to do the right things with people.

The top values that I encourage for you are:

EDUCATION
I have emphasized that education is very important. Both of you have good educations. Education opens a lot of doors for you. It is more important than anything else. Sports are all right but sports don't go very far.

RESPONSIBLE CAREERS
Cindy, you did a wonderful job as a first grade teacher for over 25 years. You have loved the kids and the kids have loved you, too. Tim, with your two degrees, you now have a very responsible job of dealing with environmental protection and the disposal of toxic waste. I am proud of both of you. I am proud of how you both have made great accomplishments in your careers.

RELATIONSHIPS
Try to make good relationships with the people that you meet. Be kind to everybody. There are too many mean people in the world today. Make friends and nurture those friendships. That goes a long way.

FAITH
Our whole family has always been church-going people. We have a lot of faith in the Lord and what He was able to do for us. I know that you, Cindy, go to church every Sunday and teach Sunday School. And, Tim, you do the same. I have always taught Sunday School in the past because faith is important. I used to be the superintendent of the young people's department. I was

very active in the church, a deacon, a trustee; a choir director, you name it.

HISTORY AND GENEALOGY

History and family heritage are valuable. I have always loved history. I got interested in it in college, sort of a minor field for me. I came to Dayton, KY when I was only one and my dad and grandfather opened the first funeral home in Dayton, Alexandria, and Florence. I have traced the family genealogy way back to 1556.

DECISIONS

Good decisions are very important because if you make the wrong ones, it will point you down the wrong path. Continue to set high goals for yourselves. Goals that you want to achieve, based upon good decisions, will keep you on the right path.

Love, Dad

Charles Tharp
Born 1925
Marketing degree from UC
Cincinnati College of Embalming
Married to Edith for 64 years
Career: Insurance and Real Estate
Dayton, KY "Historian"
Hobbies: photography, history, stamps and coins, musician

A THOUGHT FROM THE DAD'S CORNER
"If it doesn't feel right, don't do it. That's the lesson. That lesson alone, will save you a lot of grief. Even doubt means don't." **Oprah Winfrey** **Stanford Commencement Address, 2008**

To my son of age 23,

Know that: you are the most important thing in my life and that I love you more than words can ever say. But I do get frustrated with you. It seems like all you do is play video games. Some of this is probably more acceptable than my upbringing allows me to believe. But it still seems pretty excessive to me. So I am going to come straight to the point and talk about money. There are so many other things that are important as well but money seems to be a difficult issue that you and I can't agree on. You get frustrated with me and say that I focus too much on money. But here are my thoughts.

The top values that I encourage for you are:

UNDERSTAND THE VALUE OF MONEY

I have been modestly rich and I have been reasonably poor. Let me assure you, without a doubt: rich is far better.

Yes, the old cliché that is echoed by many of folk of low financial means: " *But money can't buy happiness"*. In the strictest sense that is true, but to mention only a few, it can and does buy *comfort* and *fun*. It does buy you <u>and your loved ones</u> *opportunities* that you wouldn't otherwise have. . It does allow you to have exposure to *better healthcare, nutritious and healthy foods, nice clothing, good, safe and reliable transportation, a spacious home and land for comfort and protection.* It pays for *utilities, taxes,* and *incidentals* that we often forget about until they come due. It does allow you to *travel* and *explore* what the world has to offer: to *expand your horizons* or just *rest* and *refresh your energy level* to allow you to continue your life in a productive manner. So don't lose sight of its value. Money, whether we like it or not, touches our lives in almost every way. So understand its value: understand what it can provide for you and what it cannot. Don't confuse your hobbies with your bread and butter – focus on being a good provider. There will be time later to play with your toys and hobbies. They call it

work for a reason. You are an adult now. So – be
disciplined -Grow up – stop playing the video games so
much – at least less than you are now.   Discipline is
delayed gratification – and the gratification will come.
Make good decisions. Good decisions often pay off
handsomely while bad ones usually lead to misery and
pain for yourself and those around you. To get a bit more
specific: Get the best education that you possibly can. As
difficult as it seems now – it is still usually the fastest way
to job security and growth.

Perhaps I have spent too much time at work and away
from you. I can see that in how you now treat me. It is
so hard to get the right balance in our relationship but I
am trying. I just want you to have a better life than I
have. I am just trying to do the right thing.

So I offer you this last bit of guidance. Let your
relationships be strengthened by doing the right thing
instead of trying to strengthen your relationship by doing
anything.

Love,
Dad

Anonymous
Born 1961

To my wonderful children Diana *(of age 41), and Steve (of age 38),*

Know that: my love for both of you has grown stronger over the years. You have become amazing and successful adults. Besides that, you both have become my best friends. You are great parents and have blessed me with seven wonderful grandchildren. I am extremely proud to be your dad and to be grandpa to your children. Please remember I am always here for you as long as I am able. Here are a few thoughts on living I strongly believe, hope you can find them enlightening.

The top values that I encourage for you are:

ALWAYS KEEP A POSITIVE OUTLOOK
Keep in mind that no matter how bad things may seem, there is always someone worse off than you.
Count your blessings on a daily basis.
Remember, smiles are free and the rewards are priceless.
Happiness is a choice - Always be honest.
Never be afraid to say, "I love you. I'm sorry. Thank you."
A helping hand or your presence can sometimes be the best present ever.
Judging is easier than understanding.
.

ENJOY LIFE
Laugh... Cry... Feel...Live each day.... As if it were your last.
Keep in touch with your family and friends - there is always more to learn.
Do what is right, not what is great.
It's never too late to dream - choose your love, then love your choice.
Success at home ... means success at work - Success is the journey... not the accomplishment.
Only you.... can take away your self-respect.

TREASURE THE MOMENTS
Time is not measured in seconds...but in moments - carry your camera so you can capture those moments.

Enjoy your children now and each other, they grow up too fast and time flies as you grow older.

Show them unconditional love and your support no matter what the situation.

Remember, little children have big ears – patience is a virtue –count to ten.

Let them play with the intentions to get dirty or wet….their clothes and bodies can be washed and dried.

In this busy world, make time to have quality family time. Do your best to encourage and spend one on one time with each member of your family.

Love always,
Dad

Mark Wiechman
Born 1948
Married to Margie for 42 years
LaSalle High School
Cincinnati Cooperative School of Technology- Associate Degree (Business Data Processing)
University of Cincinnati
Evening College (Administrative Management)
Computer Operator/Data Collection, Contract Administrator,
         34 years collectively.
Attorney-at-Law Assistant,
Psychology Clerk
Hobbies:
Magic/Magician – Member of:
Society of American Magicians
International Brotherhood of Magicians
(CAMAS) Cincinnati Academy of Magical Arts and Allied Sciences
Halloween-
Setting up Wiechman's Halloween Display - Count Marco's Haunted Castle Celebrating 50 yrs. 10/31/2012

To my incredible children Kayla *(of age 11)*, Nicholas *(of age 9), and* Nathan *(of age 8)*,

Know that: I love you very much, more than words or actions can ever express. Everything I do is in your best interests, as I try my hardest to exceed the wonderful job my parents did for me, in raising you. I wanted children because I think it is our duty, as God's children, to pass along the traits, both good and bad, that make us similar, but unique in our own way. Being a father to 3 wonderful children has been the hardest and most challenging undertaking of my life. The difficult balance between leading too much and letting you have your own wings, can leave one at wit's end. I can honestly say, the happiest and proudest moments of my life are when you succeed at something, be it kicking a soccer ball, getting good grades or you, just being you. The saddest moments are when I share your struggles and pain through this challenging world. Also *Know That*, I will always love you and be proud of you no matter what; no matter how high my sometimes unrealistic expectations may be, you are special to me.

The top values that I encourage for you are:

DECENCY
It may sound cliché, but the Golden Rule isn't called the Golden Rule without reason. Strive to treat everyone with the same respect you command of them. Do not judge people, or come to conclusions about people, without knowing their whole story. There are many challenging times throughout our lives where this is difficult. Don't get caught up in groups; be friends to all.

FAILURE
Two of my favorite quotes on this subject are: "In order to succeed, you must first be willing to fail." Anonymous. "Failure is the opportunity to begin again more intelligently." Henry Ford.

I ask of you, don't be afraid to fail; it is part of life. I do ask that you learn from the failures or mistake; it can make you very successful and happier in the end.

ADMITTING YOU ARE WRONG
Pride gets in the way of this. It took me 30 some years to realize the power of admitting when you are wrong. Think about it: when you admit you are wrong, you are telling someone else they are right! That makes them feel good and is powerful.

MOTIVATION, PASSION AND FAITH
I have always been fascinated with what motivates people and I think these three values go hand in hand. Usually what motivates us, is something we are passionate about, and there is no passion without faith: Faith in your religion, faith in that there are good people on this earth, faith that you are doing the right thing. Have passion and faith in everything you do, and you shall be motivated!

THE POWER OF A SMILE
It is much harder to smile than go through life with a frown. Smile often, even if you're laughing at something stupid you just did...see Failure! The same goes with making others smile: strive for it, don't ever underestimate the power of a smile. I don't think we smile enough.

Love, your Dad

NAME: Jeffrey Paul Wiley Born 1971
BS Engineering Mechanics - University of Cincinnati.
MBA - Xavier University
CAREER: 16 years at Johnson & Johnson (Ethicon Endo-Surgery) Mechanical Design and Manufacturing Engineer in NPD
HOBBIES: Golf and Sports in General.
Running Half Marathons
Assistant Coach in my children's sports.
Home projects and woodworking.

To my son of age 26,

Know that: I look back and miss so many of the parts of you growing up. There were so many times I had to choose between working and going to your events – or just sharing in the little things. Often I chose work: hopefully for the right reasons. There is so much that I could have taught you but somehow – for some reason – it never happened. Now I want to share time with you but your life is too busy. It seems to be too late for me. I have lost those precious times when you were a child. Perhaps I will be a better grandpa than father but know that I love you so much and wish I could turn back the hands on the clock.

The top values that I encourage for you are:

FAMILY
Family is so important – Be there for your wife. Be there for your children as much as you can. You will never regret being there for them. Treat the family members with respect and always be honest. Without honesty – you have no relationship. Never have clickish family secrets. These secrets are toxic and will destroy the family. Part of being a good father and husband; a good mother and wife; a good son, is being there for each other.

GOOD IMAGE
Keep up a good image – a good image sometimes opens doors – then it's up to your character to carry you through.

HALF FULL
There's good and bad in every situation: in every physical object; in every place that you look, in every second that you live. Sometimes it is easier to see the good: sometimes the bad. But both are always there. Eliminate the bad from your life whenever and wherever you can. Every bad second of time that you can eliminate from your life means that second must be good or at least neutral. At least it's not bad. This makes the good in your

life more visible. And the more good you have in your life
- well, you see the point. Life is too short to be pulled
down by the bad. Live by the Serenity Prayer the best
that you can.

PRIORITIES

Know and understand your priorities – never lose sight of
the order of your priorities. Never let a lower priority
jeopardize a more important priority. (thus the cliché –
you can win the battle but lose the war) so choose your
battles very carefully.

BE KIND

I know you are ambitious and plan to conquer the world
but do so with kindness.

"When you are kind to others, it not only changes you,
but it changes the world" – Harold Kushner

Be Generous and Compassionate

"If we always helped one another, no one would need
luck". – Sophocles

Love,
Dad

Anonymous
Born 1958

A THOUGHT FROM THE DAD'S CORNER
"Happiness is having a large, loving, caring, close-knit family in another city."
George Burns (1896 - 1996)

Continued from page 99

 Scott A. Lengle
Born 1980
Married to Brooke for 2 years
Northern Kentucky University
B.A. Speech Communication
Detective, Kentucky State Police
Hobbies and Interest: Hiking,
Camping, Competitive Pistol
Shooting, Cooking, Reading

A THOUGHT FROM THE DAD'S CORNER

Dads just want to share their advice with their kids –
so here's a tip: Just ask your dad for advice – when
he's done – ask him for the keys to the car – chances
are – he'll give them to you.

A THOUGHT FROM THE DAD'S CORNER

One of the busiest days of the year for many phone
companies is Mother's Day.
The day that most collect calls are made is Father's
Day.

CONCLUSION

Fathers often have an allowance of words, especially words of advice and guidance - and that is usually what we fathers love to give.   The allowance of words usually gets smaller and smaller as their children get taller and taller.

Sometimes it's not the message – but who delivers it, when it is delivered, and how it is delivered.

As your children read this book – be patient. Only some of what they read may be absorbed right now, but it is in writing. Keep this book open and visible. Chances are they will come back to it from time to time. It's a reference book on life.

I encourage you to talk to your children and be patient with them. Continue to look for different ways to get your message across to them- write to them if need be. Keep your doors of communication open - choose your battles very – very – very carefully. Never lose sight of your priorities.

Continue to do the next right thing...Then the next...Then the next.

Best,

R. K. Ketterer

I NEED YOUR HELP

What started out to be a rather small project, specifically for my own two daughters, grew to be something significantly larger. As fathers became aware of this concept and process, they were excited and energized by it. From there it grew – and grew exponentially.

Now I have come to realize how important and powerful this book is. I have come to understand that every person who has the status of son or daughter can learn and benefit from this book. I've broadened my focus to other children – especially children who do not always have a father's positive influence in their lives. I've come to learn that this book may be a strong positive influence in those children's lives that they may never have otherwise. There are many young people who could greatly benefit from this book.

So I solicit your help – your help to get a copy of this book into their hands. You may be one of the people who can do just that. There are many different ways this can be accomplished. You may simply pass this book onto someone that you think may benefit from it. Or you may have some means or an idea on how to get this book into the hands of the many children who desperately need a father's positive influence in their lives. If so please contact me at: www.fromthedadscorner.com

Write Your Own Page

"Every Father should be writing a page." – **James Shelton** – Retail Manager

So many of the fathers, involved in this project, have told me that this was both a challenging but very rewarding process. Gathering, organizing, and writing their deepest thoughts about life was not an easy task. But it was a very rewarding one. It is a treasure to be passed down for generations to come.

My only regret is that I will never have a page written by my own father. Often I wonder what he would have said.

And now, I encourage you fathers, to write your own page to your children, sharing with them your deepest emotional thoughts, your values, your wisdom, your experiences. The only thing stopping you is yourself. So, don't put it off. Start your page today and see it through.

You and your children will be so glad you did.

If you would like to submit your page for possible inclusion in upcoming volumes of *From The Dad's Corner* then go to www.fromthedadscorner.com.

QUICK ORDER FORM

Order information

www.fromthedadscorner.com

Contact information:

R. K. Ketterer
19 Spillman Drive
Alexandria, KY 41001

fromthedadscorner@gmail.com

859-635-8604

CPSIA information can be obtained at www.ICGtesting.com
Printed in the USA
LVOW131227161012

303025LV00001B/1/P